GOOD HOUSEKEEPING

# Making Children's Clothes

# Making Children's

# Contents

    **Introduction**    11

1    **Right from the Start**    13
*The easy way to measure a child.*
*How and where.*
*Gaining the child's interest in the project.*
*Deciding on the most suitable styles.*
*What to go for – what to avoid.*
*Suiting material to style.*
*The vexed question of children's pattern sizing.*

2    **Adjusting the Paper Pattern**    22
*How to get a perfect fit.*
*Fitting and checking without frustration.*

3    **Adapting your Patterns to Create Different Styles**    31
*How to alter basic patterns.*
*Toddlers to teenagers – how their requirements differ.*
*How to build a longer life into clothes for young children.*

| | | |
|---|---|---|
| 4 | **Equipped to Start** | 39 |
| | *Choosing and using the right 'tools of the trade' for dressmaking.* | |
| | *Getting the best out of your sewing machine.* | |
| | *Making press pads.* | |
| 5 | **Be Well Prepared** | 47 |
| | *Understanding your pattern instruction.* | |
| | *Planning economical layouts – rules of the game.* | |
| | *Right and wrong ways to cut out.* | |
| | *Methods of transferring pattern indications on to material.* | |
| 6 | **Getting the Garment Together** | 52 |
| | *Methods of tacking.* | |
| | *Suitable seams for children's garments.* | |
| | *Assembling the garment the logical way.* | |
| 7 | **Pressing Is a Priority** | 60 |
| | *Pressing isn't ironing.* | |
| | *Pressing shaped and curved seams, darts, collars etc.* | |
| | *Special fabrics.* | |
| 8 | **Dealing with Darts, Pleats, Gathers etc** | 66 |
| | *Popular ways of controlling fullness.* | |
| 9 | **The Importance of Interfacing** | 76 |
| | *How, when, and where to use woven, non-woven, and iron-on interfacings.* | |
| 10 | **Collars with Style** | 82 |
| | *Making your own collar patterns.* | |
| | *Peter Pan.* | |
| | *Collar with rise.* | |
| | *Stand-up or turn-down collars.* | |
| | *Fancy collars.* | |

| 11 | **Setting in Sleeves Professionally** | 87 |

*Plain, raglan, and magyar sleeves. Tricks to ensure success.*
*Cuffs and sleeve finishes.*

| 12 | **Openings and Fastenings** | 95 |

*Easy methods with zippers.*
*Faced and fly front opening.*
*Worked and bound buttonholes.*
*Fabric loops.*
*Hooks and eyes.*

| 13 | **Pockets Are Important** | 104 |

*Pockets that stand up to hard use.*
*Patch pockets, round and square.*
*Flap pockets.*
*Pockets incorporated in side seams etc.*

| 14 | **Hems Can Let You Down** | 109 |

*Methods of turning up straight and curved hems professionally.*
*Techniques for hems in special materials.*
*Hems in pleats etc.*

| 15 | **Coveralls, Jeans and Trousers** | 115 |

*Ideas for wet and dry play.*
*Jeans and trousers for older boys.*

| 16 | **Anoraks and Duffle Coats** | 121 |

*Making a quilted anorak.*
*Anorak with knitted bands.*
*A hooded duffle coat.*
*Finishes and fastenings.*
*Toggles and frogging.*

**17**    **How to Get that Tailor-made Look**    127
*Materials, interfacings.*
*Pad-stitching collars, revers etc.*
*Shrinking and setting in sleeves.*
*Putting in linings that last.*

**18**    **Plaids and Checks**    134
*Types of plaid.*
*How to lay up and cut correctly.*
*Avoiding difficulties.*
*Tacking, stitching, and assembling.*
*Instructions for making a kilt.*

**19**    **Ideas for Party Clothes**    141
*Ideas for girls.*
*Instructions for making a party cloak with hood from a dress pattern.*
*Ideas for boys.*
*Victorian-style velvet knickerbockers.*

**20**    **Altering and Adapting Children's Clothes**    150
*Enlarging and lengthening.*
*Ideas for altering and refurbishing.*
*Cut-downs with a difference.*

**Index**    157

# Foreword

Now that chain store clothes for children are neat and colourful, why should mothers still think it worthwhile to make their own? The answer can be summed up in one word: individuality. It's the quality found in some of the beautifully designed Continental clothes you would love your children to wear, but can't possibly afford. When you make clothes for your children, though, you have a much wider choice of style and fabric than the mass market can offer. You can add or subtract trimmings according to your own and your child's taste. You can add your own creative touches which will give a simple garment the individual look. Just as important, if the wearer's measurements aren't standard, you can adapt your pattern to give an exact fit *and* allow for future growth.

This book will help you do all this; and it includes ideas for giving outgrown or partly outworn clothes a new look and a new lease of life.

You'll find it a money-saving and enjoyable experience to follow Mrs Mordle-Barnes' suggestions and create special and individual things for your very special child.

*Jean Shapiro*
*Head of Family Centre, Good Housekeeping*

# Introduction

Making clothes for children can seldom have been more worthwhile than at present, when high labour costs make even toddlers' clothes so terribly expensive. It's also a fact that today's young mothers – and grandmothers – have less time, or inclination, for much hand sewing, tedious fittings (which children hate) and slow, out-dated ways of putting a garment together – often entailing taking it apart again!

Fortunately, modern sewing techniques and methods of assembly, based on arranging the work in logical units, have simplified the whole business, saving much time and effort. Not, however, at the expense of good workmanship or finish. . . .

This book will show you how to choose patterns and to measure your child accurately without fuss, so that you can be sure of buying the correct size. It will also show you how to perfect a basic dress, coat, and trouser pattern that can be used again and again, with minor adjustments. The simple art of adapting these perfected patterns to create any number of new styles is clearly explained, and will save you the bother and expense of buying lots of patterns.

All the important techniques needed to produce really professional results are simply described – without resort to technical jargon – and clearly illustrated. The methods chosen are particularly suitable for children's garments. We all know, only too well, how tough youngsters are on their clothes; the special hints, given throughout the book, on building in reinforcements at all points of strain will ensure a longer life for the garments you make for your children.

Other 'tricks of the trade' will show you how to avoid those all-too-common hallmarks of the amateur, such as badly set in sleeves, clumsy 'ridged' hems, thick, bulky corners, curling lapels, poorly sitting collars.

You'll find lots of ideas for party clothes for boys and girls, with the emphasis on co-ordinates; suggestions, too, for making excellent use of those remnants, picked up 'for a song', but never quite large enough to make the blouse, skirt, or whatever you originally had in mind.

Suggestions are also given for adapting and combining outgrown items to create attractive new-looking garments which will give lots of extra wear.

So, whether you are an experienced dressmaker or novice at the game, I hope that this book will help you exceed your highest expectations in enjoyment, creativity and success in making your children's clothes. And without meeting any snags or setbacks on the way!

# 1
# Right from the Start

It's a sign of the times that children – especially girls – begin to take a keen interest in their clothes at a much earlier age than children of a generation ago. Clothing manufacturers have been quick to take advantage of this, and often plan their advertising campaigns to appeal directly to the youngsters, as well as to their mothers by using combinations of clear, brash colours and eye-catching novelty trims, colourful leaflets etc.

For the mother who makes her children's clothes it's equally important to gain their interest and co-operation at the beginning of each sewing project. Otherwise, measuring and fitting can be a frustrating business for everyone, often resulting in a poorly fitting garment, especially where jackets, coats, and trousers are concerned.

Because children's measurements are constantly changing – most strikingly in length, but in girth, too, *and* in fits and starts in both directions, it is essential to keep an up-to-date list of all measurements. But do try not to let the measuring-up business become a bore to the child. Babies and toddlers seldom keep still long enough to allow you to take all the necessary measurements at one time. It's usually easier to measure a baby or toddler when in his cot, while holding his attention with 'talk' or a rhyme, while you deftly check and dot down the results. So, keep a pencil and notebook handy and seize your opportunities!

Small children will usually submit quite happily if you make a game of measuring, eg getting them to sit, stand, bend, raise arms, and so on, to a made-up rhyme (my own children really enjoyed this) but they may not oblige if merely told to do this or that! A never-failing ploy when making little girls' dresses is to make – or help her to make – a smaller edition for her favourite doll. This is also an excellent way to encourage her interest in creative sewing.

**How and where to take measurements**
For dresses, blouses, jeans, trousers, and also nightwear (this must be loose, anyway), measure the child over normal underwear. For coats, anoraks, and jackets, measure over ordinary daytime wear. Use a firm but pliable tape measure, and take all measures closely, but never tightly enough to depress the skin. A child's waistline is often undefined, so tie a ribbon or string firmly around the body resting just below the bottom rib, as a guide while measuring. Make sure the child is standing quite naturally, and not 'drawn up'. Many children tend to stick their tummies forward, and this must be taken into account when taking measurements, and also when fitting the garment.

*The measurements (figs 1a, b, and c)*

1 *Full length* from most prominent bone at

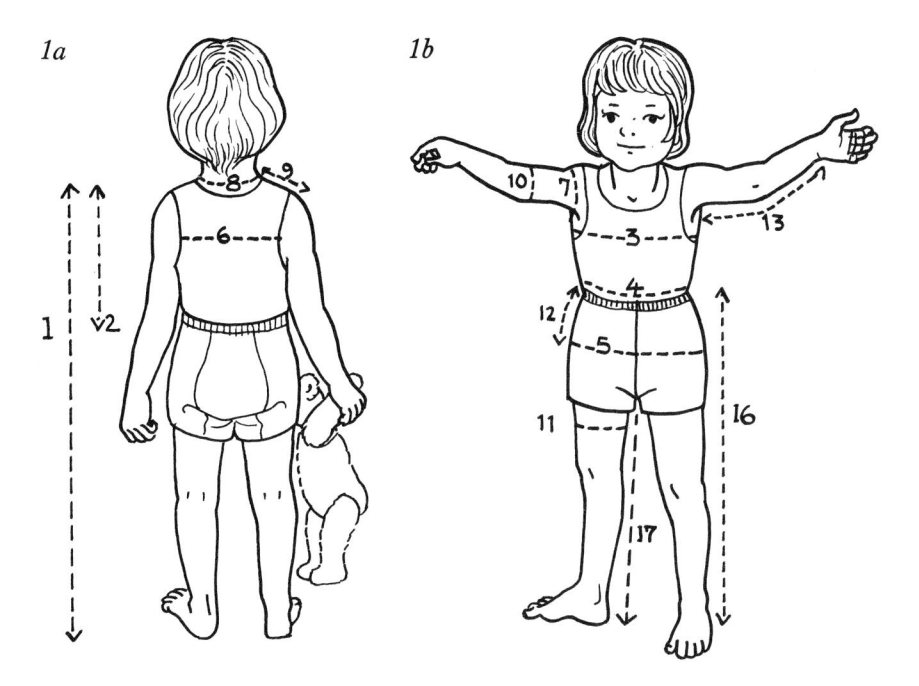

*Figs 1a, b, and c Where to take measurements*

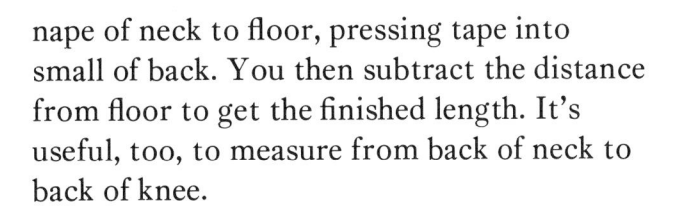

nape of neck to floor, pressing tape into small of back. You then subtract the distance from floor to get the finished length. It's useful, too, to measure from back of neck to back of knee.

2 *Neck to waist.* From nape of neck to tape around waist level.

3 *The chest.* This is taken from the back, around body over chest at 7·5 cm (3 in) below armhole.

4 *The natural waist* over ribbon or tape. (On young children, this may well be the same or more than chest measure.)

5 *Hip.* Measure around the fullest part of seat.

6 *Across the back* level with shoulder blades, midway between top of shoulder and underarm.

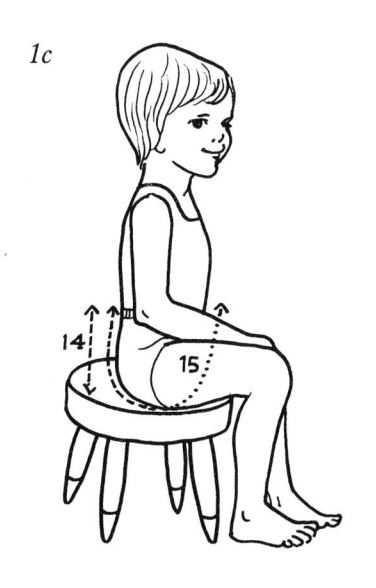

15

7 *Armhole* is taken round top of the arm close to body.

8 *Base of neck.* Measure where the neck joins the shoulders.

9 *Shoulder.* At a level in line with hollows at bottom of side neck to top of roundest part of shoulder bone.

10 *Upper arm.* Around the arm midway between shoulder and elbow.

11 *Thigh.* Measure around leg at thickest part.

12 *Waist to hipline.* From tape at side waist to actual hip bone.

13 *Long sleeve length.* From shoulder over bent elbow to bone at outside wrist.

All the above measurements are needed when making fitted garments, eg coats, blazers, jackets, princess-style dresses and anoraks, but for nightwear and simple loose fitting dresses you could omit 5, 10, 11, 12, and 13.

When making jeans, dungarees, and trousers you'll also need the following measurements, taken with a string or tape round the child's natural waist, as above.

14 *Body rise.* With the child sitting on an upright chair, measure from tape at back waist to seat of chair.

15 *Back to front waist.* Measure from tape at back waist, under the body and up to the tape at front waist.

16 *Side leg.* Measure from tape at side waist to ground, and subtract as needed.

17 *Inside leg.* From crotch to floor and subtract as needed.

**Choosing the best styles for your child**
Children's clothes have never been more practical, or so easy to wear and care for – thanks to greater understanding of children's needs and their modern life-style. It's now accepted that their clothes won't be taken care of by their wearers, but will be subjected to various kinds of ill-treatment never imposed on adult clothing. This is a point to bear in mind when choosing a style from a pattern catalogue, even though a casual browse through the pages might suggest that the choice was unlimited.

Whatever the garment you intend to make, the following points *are* worth remembering.

1 Imagine the garment on *your* child, and decide whether it will suit his or her particular build and personality. Clothes can give (or take away) a child's confidence even more than they do that of an adult. And a 'plain' child can be transformed by clothes chosen to bring out only the best features.

2 As a rule, the fewer seams and small built-in details it contains, the better the garment will look and wear. Plain, simply cut garments can be enhanced by adding collars, cuffs, braid, and other trimmings as you please. And you'll be able to try the effect without cutting or altering the garment. But keep the basic outline uncluttered.

3 Raglan and dolman-type sleeves are more comfortable than set-in ones, and will allow for growth, especially if deep, turned-up cuffs are

added. But avoid cuffs and armbands which have no openings. These can't be adjusted as the child grows. Elastic set in a slot is a good idea in suitable cases.

4 Pleated styles need more laundering and pressing than do gathers or tucks.

5 Buy extra material (self or contrasting) to make sets of collars and cuffs to be snap fastened on instead of sewn to the garment, which will look new for longer since these items wear out soonest.

6 When choosing styles for young children, avoid back fastenings, lots of fiddly buttonholes, and bows or ties. Front fastenings with zippers or Velcro can help the child to dress himself at an earlier age. Double-breasted coat and blazer styles are more easily let out than single-breasted ones, because all the buttons can be re-aligned.

**Choosing materials to suit the style**
However 'right' the chosen style, it won't look its best if made up in an unsuitable material. Yet this often happens. One sees small details attempted in bulky cloth, and attempts at tailoring in loose, flimsy materials – with equally disappointing results!

Look out for materials with strong threads in both warp *and* weft, and a smooth even weave in preference to loosely woven ones which soon catch and fray. An exception is stretch terry towelling which is ideal for young children's wear.

Small, neat patterns look best on a young child. Large designs and large checks or plaids will be distorted because of the small distances between seams and joins – besides having an overpowering effect generally. Plain colours always look well, whether dark or light, especially when relieved with contrasting trimmings, eg collars, cuffs, braid etc. Plain materials do, however, show up every mark or 'spill'. Among the best are denim, corduroy, sailcloth, and wool/Terylene or Fortrel mixtures.

Knitted synthetic materials or mixtures of natural and synthetic fibres are easy to sew, will 'give' under strain, and are lightweight and easily washed. Most are crease-resistant and need little or no pressing. But for summer clothes remember that synthetic fibres are non-absorbent, and can feel hot and uncomfortable in warm weather. Polycottons seem to be the answer here. They are cool, quickly washed and dried and need no ironing. Ginghams, too, are always popular.

For winter dresses, skirts, and coats, Terylene or Fortrel and wool mixtures combine the advantage of being warm, lightweight, and remarkably crease-resistant, too.

Many mothers are attracted by synthetic pile materials because they are so light and washable. Unfortunately the pile tends to wear thin after a while, especially at the front edges of the collar, the sleeve ends, and the pockets. It's a good idea to buy plain woven or knitted material to make matching or contrasting collars and cuffs, and to add plain bindings down the fronts. The garment will keep new-looking for twice as long.

When making jeans, dungarees, or safari-type jackets, always buy the best available quality of material. These garments have to take a lot of heavy wear, and there's a good deal of work involved in making them. A useful tip is to buy a small quantity of the same material in a different colour, to put by for later patching of seats, knees, or elbows – patches of the original colour would look too new.

## The vexed question of pattern sizing for children

Manufacturers of paper patterns in various countries have long disagreed on criteria for sizing children's patterns. There used to be wide discrepancies between patterns supposedly of the same size. In 1953 it was decided that a child's height was the most accurate guide to sizing. Not all manufacturers agreed; some preferred to base sizing on chest measurement and age. Others suggested basing infants' patterns on the child's weight. The introduction of metrication called for a reappraisal of the whole situation. The outcome has been that children's patterns, including those in the recent toddler range, are now based on breast, waist, and hip measurements *and* total height. Differences between sizes are normally 6 cm (approximately 2–4 in). Ease allowances still appear variable, but are slightly more generous than those allowed on adult patterns. So it still remains up to the individual to choose a pattern which tallies most closely to her own child's measurements. Do study the detailed information on the back of the pattern envelope – it pays off!

This is where your set of body measurements is invaluable, for, having bought your pattern by chest measurement, you can be fairly sure of a reasonable fit at neck, shoulders, and armholes (which are more difficult to alter, anyway) and can then adjust waist, hip, and all length measurements quite easily.

In view of this it's advisable to buy only patterns of a well-known make. There's no guarantee that cheap pattern offers in newspapers or magazines will be consistent in sizing or in ease allowance. I've seen some which bear no relation whatever even to the size stated on the envelope!

# 2
# Adjusting the Paper Pattern

Contrary to general belief, adjusting and adapting paper patterns to create a better fit and different styles is quite simple, and calls for no special skill. But many people seem afraid to alter a pattern in the smallest detail. When you have bought a pattern that corresponds as closely as possible to your child's measurements, take the main pieces – front, back, sleeve, and collar (if any), cut off the paper margins, and pin the pattern exactly along the seamlines, with pins parallel. Try it on over the clothing that would normally be worn under the garment.

If the pattern and style were carefully chosen, likely adjustments merely involve pleating the paper to reduce the pattern in length or width, or cutting it across in strategic positions to let in extra allowances by inserting strips of paper beneath the separated edges. Your pattern instructions show this, anyway (*figs 2a and b, 3a and b, and 4a and b*).

Children have fewer fitting problems than adults. Differences between one half of the figure and the other, hollow back or round shoulders (often due to poor posture) develop with age. Apart from the simple adjustment mentioned

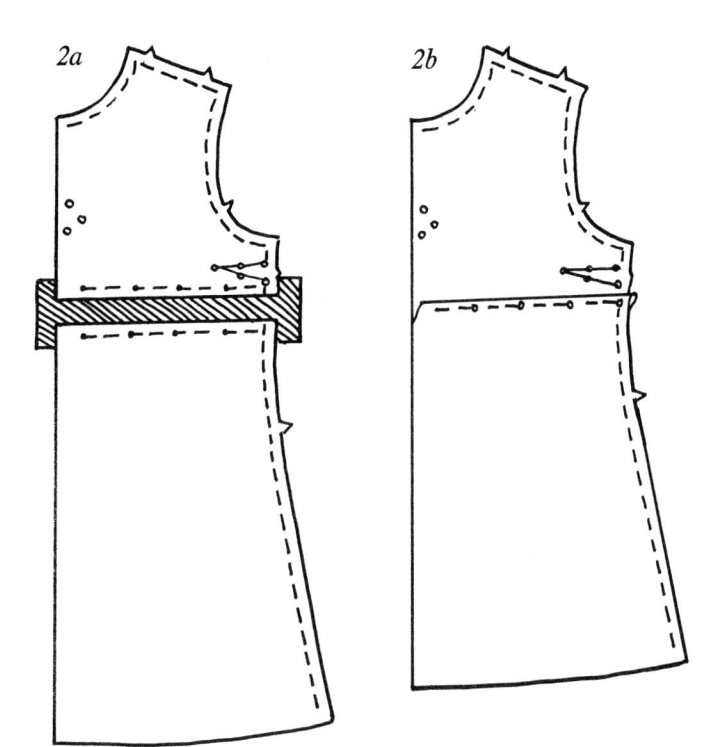

*Fig 2a Where to lengthen a pattern to suit your child's height*

*Fig 2b Where to shorten a pattern to suit your child's height*

*Fig 3a Where to lengthen a sleeve*

*Fig 3b Where to shorten a sleeve*

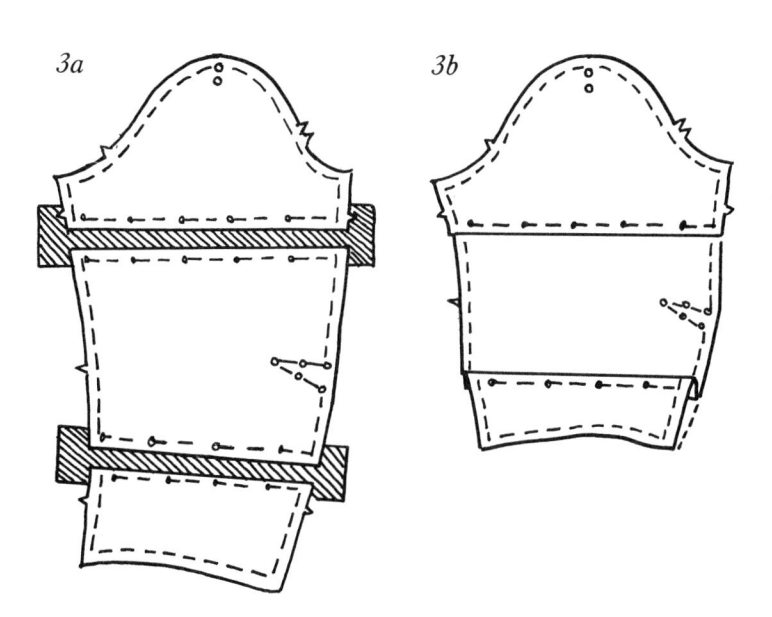

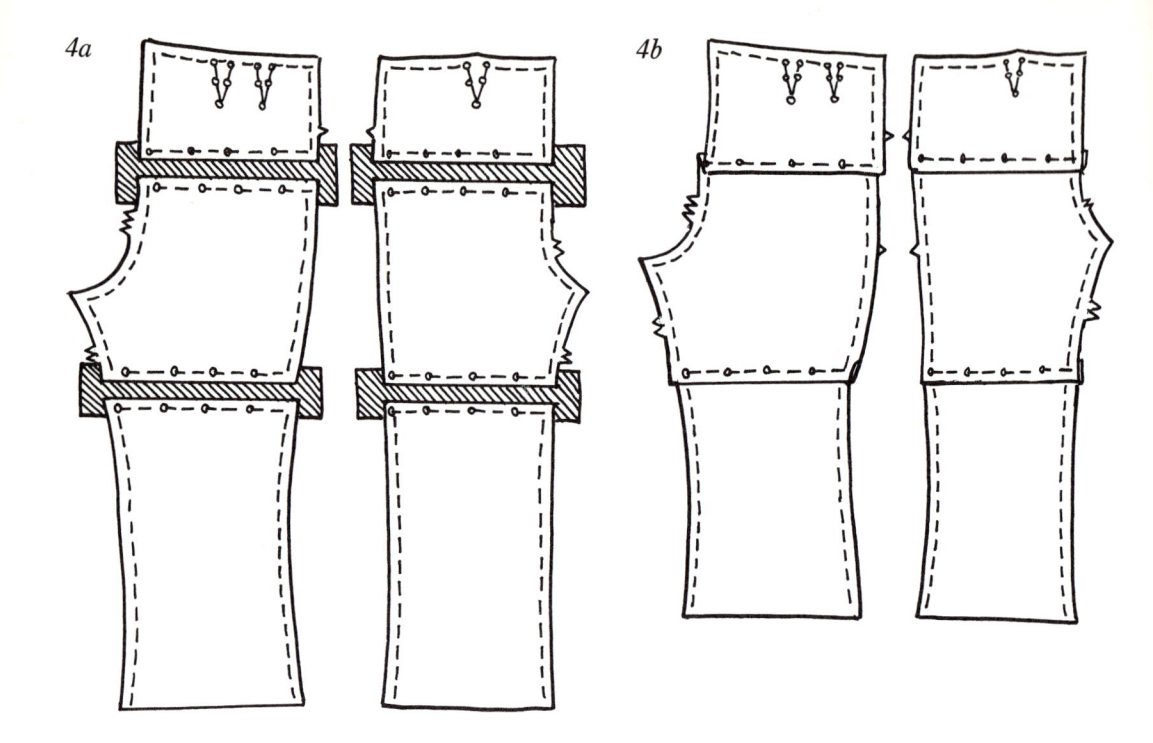

above, possible adjustments might be needed for certain pronounced characteristics, though a wise choice of style might well avoid the necessity for alterations.

*High, round tummy (figs 5a, b, and c)*
This will lift the front waistline, and make the garment shorter at front hem. On full-length dresses and coats with no waist seam, the garment will stand right out from the body in front, with a lifted hem. On a bodice, add on as necessary at centre front waistline, and slope off to the original line at side seams. On one-piece dresses or coats, a small dart may be taken out of the side seams on the front(s) just above hip level. If hem is still shorter in front, add sufficient at centre of hemline to make it level, tapering off to nothing at side edges.

*Fig 4a Where to lengthen trousers*

*Fig 4b Where to shorten trousers*

*Fig 5a Normal pattern on child with high tummy*

5a

*Figs 5b and c How to adjust pattern for a high tummy*

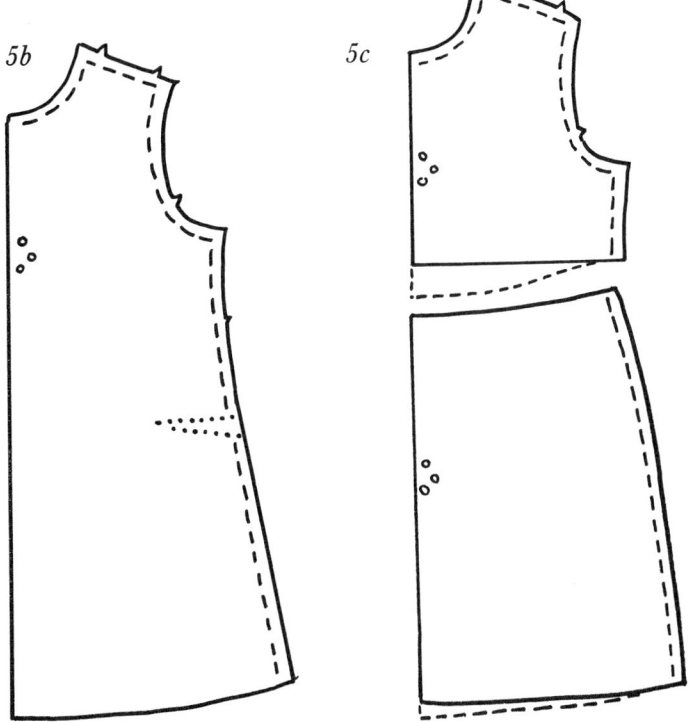

5b

5c

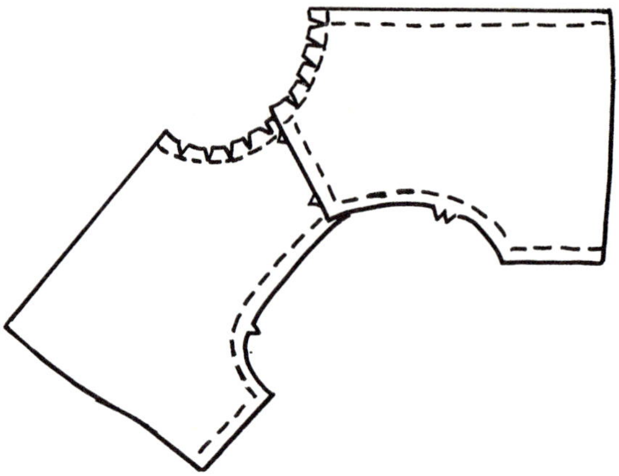

*Fig 6 How to enlarge a tight neckline*

*Tightness at neck (fig 6)*
For the small child with a rather short, chubby neck, fitted collars and button-up-to-the neck styles can be highly uncomfortable – if even slightly too high or too tight. But when trying on the pinned-up pattern the neck may at first appear too tight merely because the turning allowance has not been clipped at frequent intervals down to within 1 cm ($\frac{3}{8}$ in) of marked seamline. So, before trying on, pin back and front patterns together with seamlines meeting at shoulder and underarm and measure round the actual stitching line with the tape measure on its edge. Double the score and test this on the child. If too tight, draw a new sewing line on pattern slightly below the original one. Clip the paper turnings at 2 cm ($\frac{3}{4}$ in) intervals, and try pattern on. Be wary of cutting neck too low – a little makes a lot of difference on curved measures! If garment has a collar, enlarge this to correspond with new measurement.

*A rather thin neck (fig 7)*
A too loose or too low neck is easy to adjust on the pattern but extremely difficult to rectify once

*Fig 7 How to take in a loose neckline*

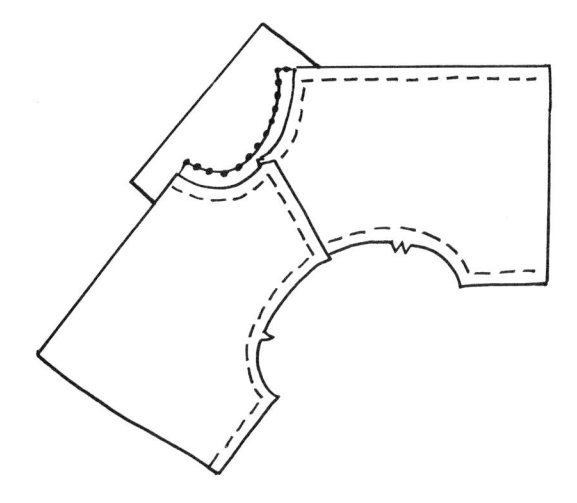

it is cut out in material. Pin front and back patterns together as above, and try on the child. Measure the distance from seamline of neck to position where you want it to be on the child. Remove pattern and unpin underarm seam. Place front and back flat over a sheet of plain paper. Hold pattern down with pins, and redraw new neckline as required, allowing normal turnings. (Remember to adjust collar or neck facings to correspond.)

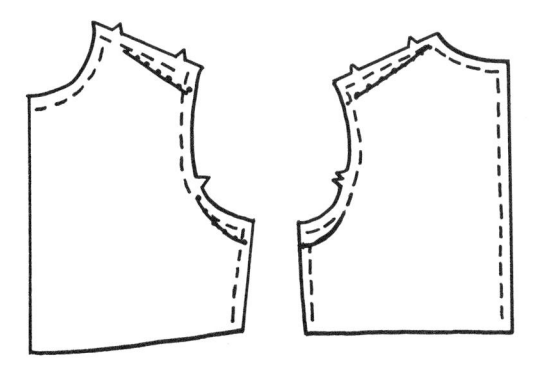

*Sloping or narrow shoulders (figs 8a and b)*
These can cause every garment to look very sloppy and ill-fitting, but even a slight adjustment on the pattern can make all the difference here. Pin bodice together on exact shoulder and

*Fig 8a How to adjust for sloping shoulders*

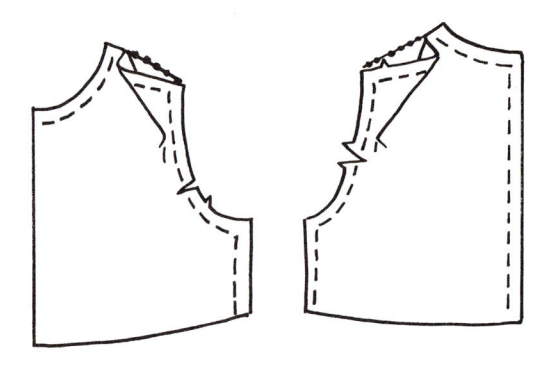

*Fig 8b How to adjust for narrow shoulders*

underarm fitting lines, and try on the child. Pinch up the edges of pattern along shoulder, and insert pins on natural line of slope. Mark new line and trim off surplus allowance. If the shoulders are too wide, don't cut off at top of armhole as this will spoil the line. Instead, take up a small slanting pleat in back and front bodice to bring armhole seamline over top of shoulder bone. Taper pleats down to nothing to enable the pattern to lie flat, clip the armhole edge, and correct the line.

*Adjustments for jeans or trousers (figs 9a and b)*
It is essential that these garments should fit really comfortably as well as looking smart and well cut. There should be enough room over the crotch area – even though older children insist on the tight-fitting look. These two factors aren't incompatible. It's mainly a matter of the intersecting seams being in exactly the correct position. The garment can look snug over seat and stomach and have close fitting upper legs, and still be comfortable when moving or sitting down. Here, as with a dress or jacket, it is worthwhile taking trouble to get a basic pattern that is perfectly adjusted to your child's figure.

Don't attempt to try on paper patterns for

jeans and trousers. The pattern is sure to get torn, and it's also important to test while the child is sitting down. The most satisfactory way is to trace the pattern on to some plain material or old sheeting. To ensure accuracy, spread the material flat on a table over a thickness of blanket and iron the pattern over this. Mark out all seamlines, darts etc on the material, turning pattern over and repeating on second half. Cut out, and stitch up side seams, inner leg seams and front-to-back seam, leaving enough open in front for easy trying on. Clip turnings at inner curve in crotch area to release. The length from the back waist to crotch junction is all-important. Also if the curve of the centre back seam is too generous the seat will bulge; if too straight, the crotch will be dragged towards the back causing discomfort and horizontal creases across the front. Check this carefully when trying on the mock-up. See

*Fig 9a How to lengthen the back of trousers*

*Fig 9b How to shorten the back of trousers*

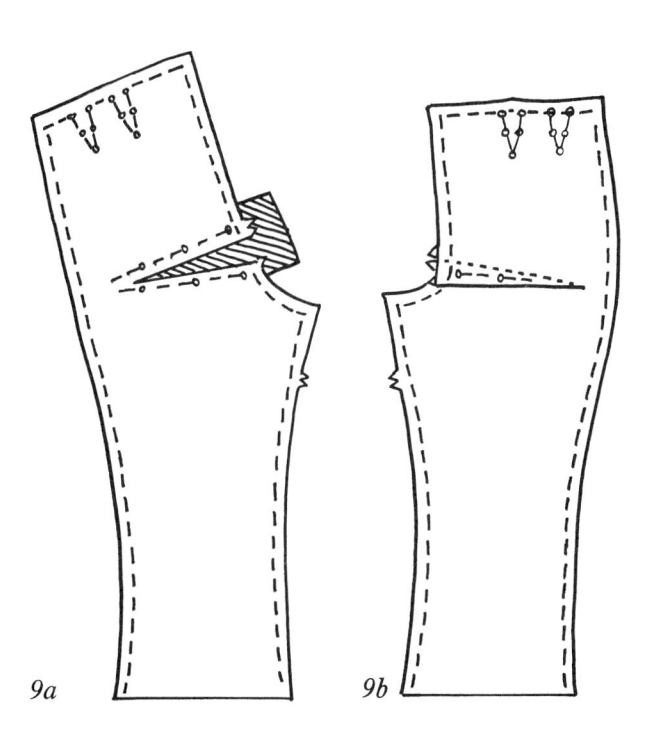

that the side seams run straight, and there are no deep creases at the back, from crotch diagonally down the legs.

With the child sitting down, make sure there is sufficient accommodation for comfort, and check that back and front waist are level with natural waistline – except in the case of hipsters. Note down any alterations required, and record these on the material after taking the seams out so you can use the corrected trousers as a pattern for cutting the actual material, and also as a basis for future adaptations of style. Re-curve lines distorted by taking up pleats, or letting out.

*Keeping a set of tested patterns for reference*
This will save endless time and trouble. When you have perfected for your child a simple basic dress, coat (or jacket), also a sleeve, and jeans pattern as described, it's worthwhile cutting out the main pieces of these in non-woven interfacing, with all essential indications marked in ball point or crayon, eg seamlines, darts, pocket positions etc. As the child grows it's simple to enlarge the patterns by adding on or letting in extra interfacing as described. Small extra allowances of up to 2 cm ($\frac{3}{4}$ in) may be added on to side seams without upsetting the balance of the garment. And, of course, side seams of sleeves must also be increased by the same amount to equalize armhole size.

This set of tried and tested patterns can also be adapted to make any number of other styles, so saving the expense of buying a large number of patterns, all of which consist basically of the same thing, and each possibly having to be adjusted to achieve a perfect fit.

# 3
# Adapting your Patterns to Create Different Styles

The principles of pattern adapting are similar to the techniques described for adjusting patterns – eg slashing; spreading and pinning the relevant pieces on to plain paper; and marking new seamlines, dart pockets and buttonhole positions. Style lines and other features may be added as you please, providing the basic shape and size of the overall pattern are maintained.

When planning to adapt a pattern, first make a sketch of the new style to get an idea of the best proportions. Then, working on a good flat surface, and with a roll of white kitchen paper or large sheets of plain paper, pins, sticky tape, crayons, and paper scissors at hand, lay out the main pieces of the pattern over the paper and sketch in the new lines and features. The examples below will give an idea of the many different adaptations you can easily make from a child's plain dress pattern without a waist seam.

*Fig 10 Dress with a high yoke*

1. A high yoke, shaped or plain (*fig 10*).

2. A bodice to the natural waistline or to the hipline (*fig 11*).

3. A straight, slightly flared or very full skirt, as for a skating skirt (*figs 12a, b, c, and d*).

4. A skirt gathered on to the bodice.

5. Pleats could be introduced – box, knife, inverted, wide, or narrow. You might prefer one central pleat, one each side, or the entire skirt pleated (*figs 13a and b*).

*Fig 11 Dress with a bodice to the natural waistline*

Figs 12a, b, c, and d How to make a flared skirt

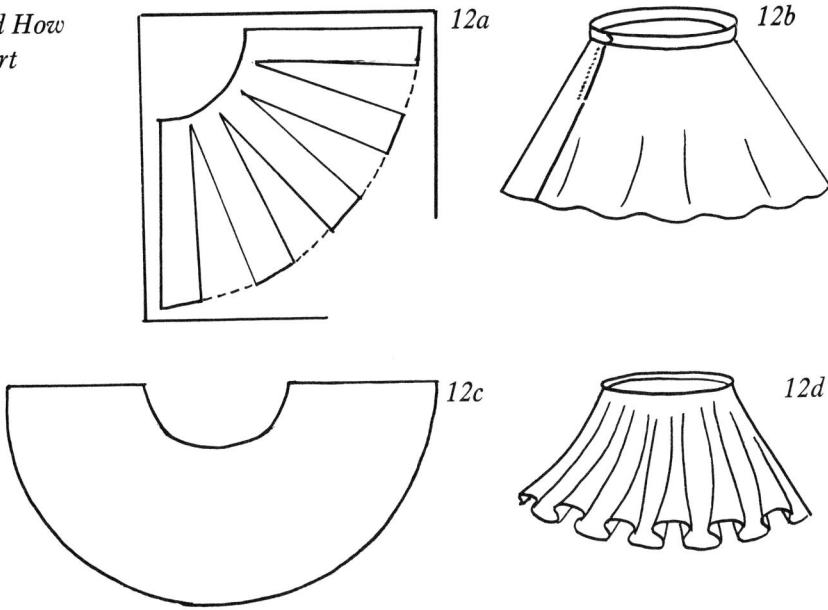

6 Fullness can also be introduced by rows of close tucks, or smocking at the bodice, or in a wide band at the chest or waist, according to how much extra fullness you want.

By adding fullness from the shoulder from a small yoke, a dress pattern, shortened, can be used as a basis for various types of blouse pattern. You can also use a plain dress pattern to

Figs 13a and b How to make a pleated skirt

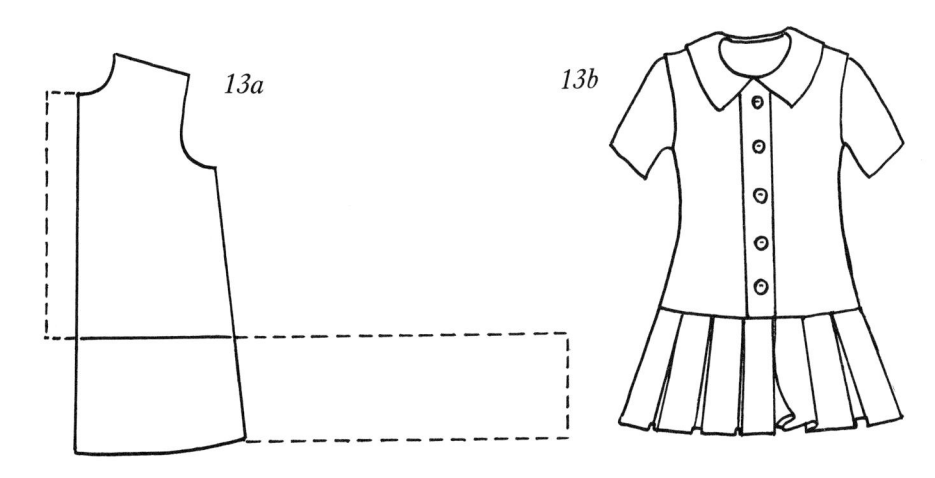

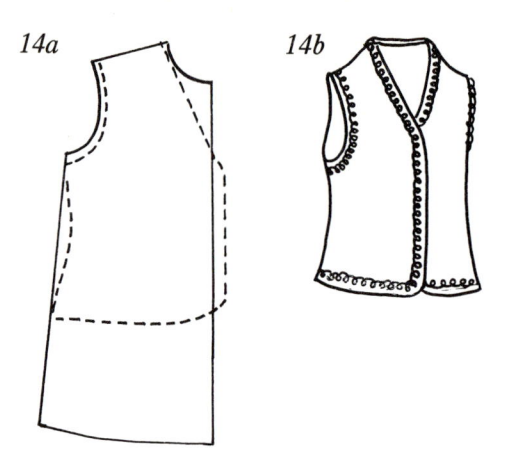

*Figs 14a and b Making a jerkin pattern*

make patterns for waistcoats, jerkins (*figs 14a and b*), tunics, and tabards. The same dress pattern could become a button-through style, merely by slashing down the centre front (on a whole front) and adding overwrap and facing allowances to cut edges.

To make a princess-line dress (*figs 15a, b, c, and d*), draw the style or panel seams on the front and back patterns, and pin the separated parts on to paper. The desired amount of flare is added below the waistline as shown in *figs 15b and c*. Pleats can also be incorporated into the panel seams.

*Figs 15a, b, c, and d Adapting a pattern to make a princess-line dress*

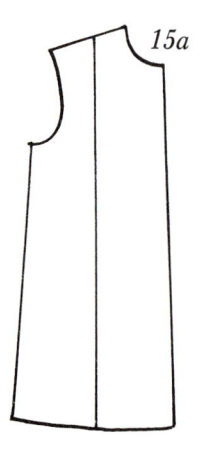

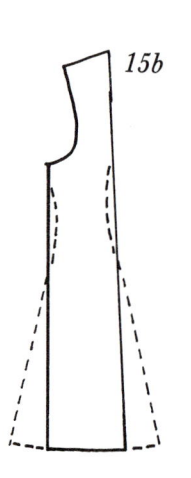

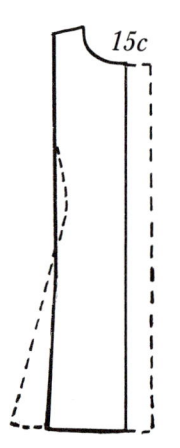

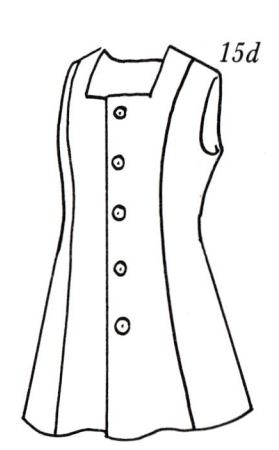

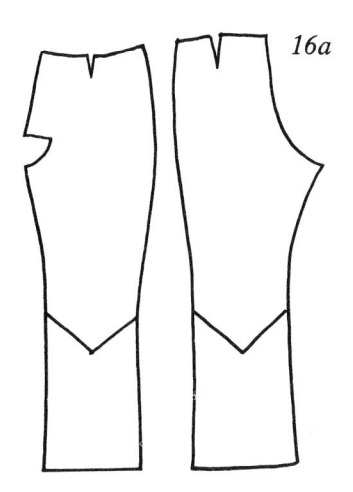

*Figs 16a, b, and c Making flared jeans*

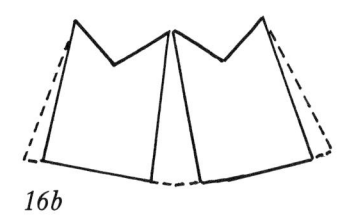

Similarly, a plain coat or jacket pattern may be manipulated – though in a more restricted way – to give a yoked style, or to add a back pleat. Here too, panel seams can be introduced to add more flare, as for a simplified riding jacket. However, always consider the thickness of the cloth and its texture when planning the amount of extra seaming to be added, or the coat could look cumbersome and overworked. As a general rule, the thicker or fluffier the material, the fewer the seams and the less detail it will take.

Jeans and trousers patterns are equally capable of providing many variations of style (*figs 16a, b, and c*). Here are a few examples:

1 Add extra flare from the hips for bell-bottoms, or from the knee only.

2 Add a diagonal style seam from below the knee (this can often save material when laying out the pattern).

3 Shorten for bermuda or short-shorts, with or without turn-ups.

4 Add wide turn-ups in contrasting material.

5 Make a shaped hip yoke, possibly incorporating pockets.

6 Adapt a jeans pattern to make a boiler suit or dungarees.

Capes and various collars can also be made by using the front and back patterns of a dress or jacket. (See chapter 10.) These, with the addition of cuffs, belts, and pockets will transform a garment without altering the basic pattern.

A plain sleeve pattern can be used as the basis for several other types of sleeve. The pattern is divided up and slashed and opened to produce:

1 Extra fullness for a gathered head.

2 A full flare for gathering the bottom into a cuff (bishop sleeve).

3 A raglan sleeve, with or without an overarm seam.

It's best to begin with quite simple adaptations, eg adding a yoke, and introducing one or two pleats or fullness into the skirt. As you gain confidence, you can go on to more complicated styles. When slashing the pattern to make a new seam, always remember to add normal turnings to *both* cut edges. First test out the effect by pinning the pattern together before attempting to cut it out in cloth, to make certain that the new seams come exactly where you intended them to be.

**Toddlers to teenagers –
how their requirements differ**
Until recently, the styles of toddlers' and tiny children's clothes were most conservative, and had scarcely changed in a generation. There was

a firm tradition of pastel colours, smocked bodices, and puff sleeves – often gathered into tight little bands allowing for no natural growth! Tiny girls' dresses had the inevitable high yoke and gathered skirt. Little boys wore shortened versions over matching 'trousers' or 'buster suits' with checked shirt and plain shorts attached by up to eight awkward little buttons! Even for babies, the traditional layette has largely given way to cotton or synthetic knitted all-in-one garments which stretch comfortably as the baby grows.

Now, almost anything goes – dark colours or brilliant ones, with styles that are miniature copies of those worn by older brothers and sisters. The mother who sews has far more scope for originality and innovation. Even so, there remain certain basic requirements for toddlers' and young children's clothing. Most important of these are:

1 Lots of room – especially over the seat area.

2 Ample armholes, preferably raglan-style.

3 Extra long openings, at neck and elsewhere, with quick and easy fastenings.

Materials need to be smooth and supple; flat seams are to be preferred to French seams wherever possible.

At this stage, clothes must stand up to endless washings rather than actual rough wear. Garments are usually outgrown before outworn. Here are some ways to build longer life into toddlers' and young children's clothes:

1 Make side fastenings with extra wide overwraps. Sew on snap fasteners, no 3 size.

As the child grows, unpick and move the lower halves as required.

2 Substitute shoulder fastenings for front openings. Wide overwraps can be similarly adjusted later.

3 Make wide tucks on the inside at waist seam or in the skirt, and add ric-rac braid over the join outside. This will prevent a 'rubbed' line from showing when the tuck is eventually let out.

4 Choose pinafore or tabard-type overdresses, worn over shirts or knitted jumpers. Make wide allowances on shoulders, and move buttons as needed.

5 Make trousers with 5 cm (2 in) tucks on the inside below waist slot, and make turn-ups which can be turned down later.

6 Long sleeves can be cut off and given a turn-up for short sleeves. A little thought when planning clothes that can be adapted without trouble pays off every time!

The same applies to older children, though here the choice of materials is wider. Schooldays bring more rough and tumble, and tougher cloth is called for. Knitted fabrics get pulled – holes appear; buttons are wrenched off, pockets pulled out, and often clothes really *have* had it by the time they are outgrown. (See chapter 20.) Even so, it's worth making these clothes with an eye to letting down, using simple expedients like those mentioned above. Not all children are so hard on their clothes!

# 4
# Equipped to Start

Making children's clothes calls for the same high performance from your 'tools of the trade' as when sewing something ambitious for yourself. Before starting on a project, check your equipment carefully.

*Sewing machine*
Make sure that your machine is working perfectly, is dust-free, well – but not too well – oiled, giving a perfect stitch and tension. It should run quietly and smoothly without vibration, irrespective of its age or type. Well maintained machines of thirty or forty years ago are still giving efficient service. But if yours is a modern automatic or semi-automatic model, don't begrudge time spent in mastering its intricacies, especially any special procedures you intend to use on a particular garment, eg buttonholes, tucking, blind-hemming, or embroidery. Have a trial run on spare material, and make sure that your machine is fitted with the right sized needle for the job, which is really sharp. Needles need renewing more often than most people think!

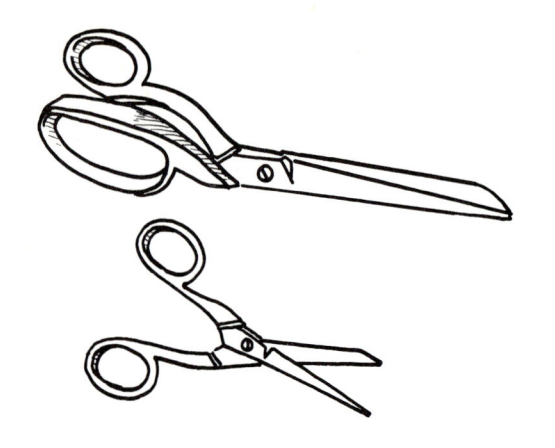

*Fig 17a Cutting out scissors*

*Fig 17b Trimming scissors*

## Scissors

Next in importance come scissors. Get the very best. Cut-price scissors are never a bargain. You'll need at least two pairs, kept safely away from the children, and used for no other purpose. First, a pair of 20·5 cm (8 in) or 23 cm (9 in) shears, with a shaped grip for the fingers (*fig 17a*), and a 12·5 cm (5 in) pair for trimming down, levelling seam edges etc (*fig 17b*). Additionally, a 10 cm (4 in) pair with needle-sharp points for clipping and snipping is extremely useful. For paper cutting and pattern adaptation, an old pair of medium-sized scissors is invaluable.

The blades of scissors should move slightly stiffly against one another for best results. In time, they'll probably loosen, but a turn of the screw in the middle will tighten them again.

## Needles

Hand needles vary in length and thickness, according to their purpose. Keep a good selection, and pick the right one for each job. I've known people who boast of using one old bent favourite for almost everything! Two types are used in dressmaking – sharps and straws. Straws are used by experienced dressmakers because they facilitate speedy and skilled work. They are longer, proportionately, than sharps. Sizes 9 and 10 are used for fine work; no 8 for general purposes, and nos 6 and 7 for thick materials. Get packets of the sizes you most use – not assorted sizes in one packet, most of which you'll probably never use.

With machine needles, too, be sure you have the right size and type for each job. Sizes 11 (60–70), 14 (80–90), and 16 (100) are the most commonly used.

Besides the normally pointed machine needles, you can now get special needles for sewing Courtelle and other knitted fabrics. These have a ball point, which parts but does not pierce the knitted structure. Ask for Singer no 2020 or the equivalent in other makes. Also available are 3-bladed machine needles for sewing the ever popular soft suedes and light leathers for clothing (Singer no 2033). These are stocked at Singer shops and you will find other brands in department stores.

*Pins*

Always buy steel dressmaker's pins – never the plated kind. Steel pins will rust if not kept in a dry place; place a sugar lump in the box to absorb any moisture. Plated pins are thick, with blunt points, and cause ugly holes in fine materials. Pins 2.5 cm (1 in) long are usual, but fine 'lillikins' only 6 mm ($\frac{1}{4}$ in) are ideal for use with fine chiffons etc.

*Tape measure and rulers*

A good tape measure is essential. You can buy the glazed linen type with metal ends, and measurements on both sides. Limp ones soon stretch and are unreliable. Spring tape measures housed in fancy containers are pretty useless, too. Being narrow, they soon stretch and twist. The steel spring measures (*fig 18*) are a better buy. You'll also need a long (metre) and a short ruler for ruling lines, measuring from floor to hemline etc.

*Fig 18 Steel tape measure*

*Threads*
As a general rule, use threads made from the same source as the yarns in your material, eg pure silk yarn with silk, cotton with cottons, synthetic threads (Drima, Dual Duty, Trylko, etc) with man-made fibres. However, many fabrics are mixtures of natural and synthetic yarns, and here you will use the thread you consider most appropriate. But do not use synthetic thread for any garment which will be ironed or pressed with a hot iron, or the thread may melt and the garment literally fall apart! Thread sizes are 60–50 for fine work, 40 for general use, and 30 for heavy materials.

Keep at hand a good supply of tacking thread of average (40) thickness, and avoid coarser varieties sold for the purpose, as these can spoil the turnings by leaving ugly holes. To prevent thread tangling, keep a piece of beeswax (*fig 19*) handy. Just rub thread over it.

*Fig 19 Flat piece of beeswax*

*Thimble*
A well fitting thimble of silver, steel, or bone is a 'must' for serious sewers. For tailoring, where sensitive finger-tip manipulation is necessary, you can buy special thimbles with open tops.

*Chalk etc*
Have two or three pieces of tailor's chalk (*fig 20*)

*Fig 20 Tailor's chalk*

*Fig 21 Stiletto*

in different colours, for marking. Also crayon pencils for pattern adjustment and adaptation.

*Stiletto*
A useful tool for making holes for worked eyelets (*Fig 21*).

*Triangle and set square*
Made of clear plastic, and useful for marking grain lines, bias, and for pattern adaptations.

*Sewing gauge*
A handy gadget in plastic or metal with a sliding marker, for measuring hem depths, pleat and buttonhole spacings, scallops etc.

*Bodkin*
For threading ribbon and elastic.

*Unpicking tool*
Invaluable for unpicking seams. Some have a scarlet 'blood spot' where the cutting edge begins. If yours doesn't, use it carefully – it's easy to cut too far into the fold edges of the material.

*A magnet*
This is tremendously useful, especially as the children will be eager to pick up any stray pins and needles with it!

*Sticky tape*
This is useful, too, for holding materials together when pins might be harmful, as a guide for top-stitching, holding zippers in place etc. But *don't* use it on loosely woven or 'loopy' materials. Removing the tape could damage the threads.

Fig 22 Tracing wheel

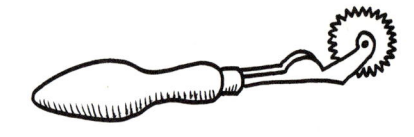

*Tracing wheel*
Used for marking seamlines, outlines etc through on to a layer of paper underneath when adapting patterns (*fig 22*).

*Dressmaker's paper and plain kitchen paper*
These are needed when altering or adapting patterns.

*Pincushions*
These come in various shapes, but the most handy is a small wrist pincushion (*fig 23*). Equally useful is a similar one to hang on to the reel holder which most machines have.

Fig 23 Wrist pincushion

*Tweezers*
These are handy for pulling out threads and tailor tacks.

*Waste bin or box*
Dressmaking can be an untidy hobby, so save yourself extra work by dropping in all waste pieces, clippings, and thread-ends straight away. The habit soon becomes automatic!

*A full-length mirror*
This is a tremendous help when trying on children's clothes – they're much more likely to be interested if they can see themselves in the mirror. A cross reflection will often change to a laughing one, I've found!

*A hem marker*
This is a time saver. The type with a rubber bulb which squirts French chalk in a fine line often proves an attraction to a fidgety child.

*Cutting board*
One of the newer dressmaking aids is a folding hardboard cutting surface, marked out in squares. This is a help, too, when making pattern adaptations, enabling you to draw straight and diagonal lines quickly and accurately from marked lines on to your pattern.

Having collected all your smaller items of equipment, keep them together in a strong workbox or small attaché case. And, if your children are young, well up and out of reach! Older children, too, often have a habit of raiding Mother's sewing box, and using these items – to their detriment – for highly unorthodox purposes!

*Pressing equipment*
Whenever you're dressmaking, keep your iron and ironing board at the ready, together with several pressing cloths of different thicknesses. The *ironing board* should be firm and steady, with a really safe rest for the iron. Many accidents have happened to children through knocking against the ironing board and sending the iron sliding off a too-precarious rest. The ideal iron is a medium-weight model with heat settings. This will deal adequately with light, medium, and fairly heavy materials. Choose a steam model instead – if you don't mind their extra bulk. For babies' and children's dressmaking, a tiny travelling iron is ideal for coping with the smaller details – collars, little sleeves etc. You'll need a *sleeve board*, too (*fig 24*).

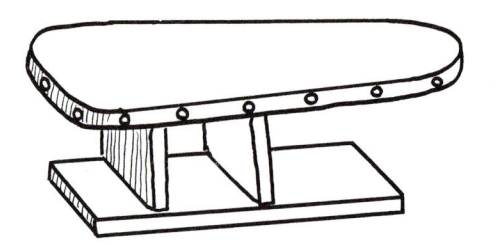

*Fig 24 Sleeve board*

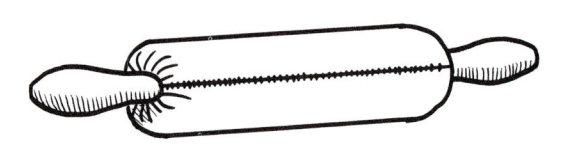

*Fig 25 Padded roller*

For really professional results, you'll need a *padded roller* (*fig 25*) for pressing seams apart without leaving an impression, and a *shaped press pad* for darts, sleeve tops, collars. Here's how you make them. Pad a wooden rolling pin with a layer of cotton, Terylene or Fortrel wadding, cover with white calico or sheeting and finely stitch up the join. For the shaped press pad, cut two pieces of calico (*fig 26*). Sew it up, leaving 5 cm (2 in) open on straight of material – not on the bias. Turn it to right side, and stuff *very* firmly with sawdust before oversewing the opening. The pad must be really hard to be effective. Foam chips or soft fillings, eg kapok, are too soft.

With this equipment, every garment you make for your children should be a pleasure, and a success.

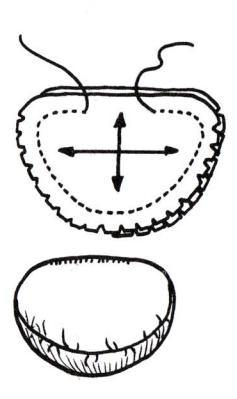

*Fig 26 How to make a shaped press pad*

# 5

# Be Well Prepared

The more experienced the dressmaker, the more time she'll willingly devote to studying the pattern instruction sheets before starting to cut out. She knows it pays off!

So many setbacks occur because some statement or symbol has been overlooked or misunderstood in the hurry to start on the garment. Nowadays, only cheaper makes of pattern rely on perforations to convey vital information on grain direction, seam allowances, pocket positions, darts etc. Well-known makes all have full instructions printed clearly on each pattern piece, with diamond-shaped outward notches as a warning not to snip into the turnings. These notches are single, double, or treble, and make it a quick and easy job to match pieces. But on frayable materials the notches soon disintegrate and become indistinguishable. In such cases they should all be tailor tacked. A point often overlooked is the numbering of notches on some patterns. This is a helpful device to show the order in which the seams should be stitched. Another symbol sometimes ignored is the arrow found on stitching lines which shows the direction of stitching each seam.

Double cutting lines show just where to insert the scissors, but many dressmakers prefer to remove the margins first. This makes for economical laying up.

After studying all the symbols, and ringing around the correct layout for your child's sizes, the width of material you have, and chosen view, pick out all pattern pieces not applicable, and return them to the pattern envelope at once. This can save many a mistake!

## Preparation of material

Spread out the material and examine it closely for any marks, flaws or pulled threads, and indicate these with coloured threads so you can avoid them when laying up the pattern. See that the cut edges are absolutely on the grain – they seldom are – and pull up a crosswise thread to use as a cutting guide. (You needn't pull it right out.) Sometimes material is cut on the grain, but the material appears 'out of true' as it lies on the table. If so, get someone to help you to pull the weave back into line, and press the material if necessary. Hold one end each – and pull!

Unless marked pre-shrunk (usually along the selvedge), pure wool needs to be damp-shrunk before using, as explained in chapter 7.

## Planning a layout

Although you will normally follow the appropriate layout shown for the size, width of material and chosen view shown on the printed diagram, there are times, especially when making children's clothes, when you may be using a remnant, and have to plan your own layout to the best advantage. Here are some hints to help you:

1 If possible, work on the double. Always place the larger pieces on first, with their widest edges, eg hem, to the cut edge, filling in with smaller ones.

2 Always place patterns on the correct grain line – never 'off the straight' unless indicated. Sometimes, on a plain, square weave with no pile or pattern, you can place collars, cuffs, and occasionally sleeves and facings *across* the weave instead of along it, if you are really short of material.

3 If material has a nap, furry pile, or one-way pattern, all pieces must run in the same direction. No space-saving dovetailing is possible.

4 Place patterns with selvedge threads running down bodices, skirts, slacks, sleeves (except as mentioned above), and frills; belts, too, except on a strong square weave which won't stretch on the weft.

5 Facings can be deceptive. All-in-one armhole facings take a lot of material. Save on these by halving the pattern on the straight grain, and adding turnings to each half. Long front facings which widen out and include the front neck can also be separated somewhere below the shaping (but avoiding buttonhole positions) and turnings can be added. The unshaped strips can often be accommodated alongside the main piece at the selvedges.

    Where material is short, facings can be cut from matching lining material, and collars, cuffs, and belts from contrasting material.

6 Sometimes you can save by folding material across its width. But, there's a warning here! Except on plain material with no pile or

49

pattern be sure to cut across the fold, and turn the under piece around, so both layers run the same way, with right sides facing. Otherwise, the pile or pattern on the lower layer will be reversed – with disastrous results.

7 If it's impossible to arrange all the pattern pieces on the folded width, try with the material opened out flat, but remember that each piece must be laid out twice, with second halves reversed. To prevent mistakes, it's wiser to cut each half again fastening it to the original wherever an edge is marked 'fold'. If a skirt pattern is too wide, you can't join pieces on – unless the join can be concealed in a pleat or underwrap. Introducing a centre front or back seam may help sometimes. It will at least look intentional!

8 Never – but never, skimp on turning allowances or hems. Try several layouts first, and make a sketch of the one that works out best. With experience, you'll develop considerable skill in achieving space-saving layouts.

**Cutting out**

Lay the material on the table, smooth it carefully, and pin the selvedges together at frequent intervals (except on opened out material).

If the pattern pieces are creased, iron them. They'll lie against the material as if magnetized! Following the chosen layout, arrange the pieces as indicated. Insert steel pins within the turning allowance and diagonally across all corners. Check every piece with the diagram before actually cutting out.

Cut with really sharp scissors, using the large shears for long main lines and the smaller ones for corners, curves, and cutting notches outwards. This ensures more accurate cutting and cleaner lines than you can obtain with just the one pair. Except when cutting out linings or dress felt, don't use pinking shears. They cut less accurately, and eat into the turnings. (As a seam finish, they are useless, anyway, as the edges soon fray out in wear.) Cut out with long, clean strokes, using the full length of the blades, and never lifting the lower blade from the cutting surface. Cut all notches outwards, but on thick materials mark these with tailor tacks instead. On pieces which are cut against the fold, eg backs, collars etc, make a tiny snip at either end of fold to indicate dead centre.

Often no special pattern is given for interfacings, so cut these from the appropriate pattern pieces, and, if woven, on exactly the same grain.

**Tacking and marking**
After cutting out the pieces, leave pins in until all sewing lines, darts, pocket positions, buttonholes etc have been tailor tacked, or marked on both layers. Don't skimp on the tacking. It's the blueprint for accurate assembly, and certainly saves much time later on. For quick identification of the various symbols when making up, use different coloured threads for tacking, eg white for seamlines, blue for darts, green for buttonholes, and so on – and keep to this arrangement for all your dressmaking.

Always keep the larger cuttings. They may be needed at some future time for repairs, or for invisibly mending a tear with a thread from the actual material of a garment.

# 6
# Getting the Garment Together

Assembling the garment will present no unforeseen snags provided that:

1 The pattern has been tried on the child, adjusted where necessary, and tested.

2 All essential indications, ie buttonholes, pocket, pleat, and dart positions, have been transferred on to your material, together with all notches and seamlines, preferably with different colours for each.

There are various ways of doing this, according to the type of material.

*Tailor tacking (figs 27a, b, and c)*
This is very reliable, since both halves (sleeves, fronts, collars etc) are bound to be identical. Use a long – up to a metre – double thread, and take a small stitch through both layers of material; then pull thread up, leaving a loop big enough to pass

27a

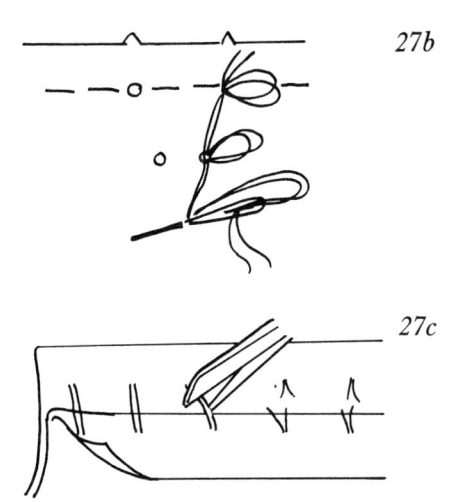

*Figs 27a, b, and c Tailor tacking*

your thumb through; take second stitch over first. Cut the thread 2·5 cm (1 in) from material. For a continuous line of tacks, don't cut, but proceed to next mark. Cut *between* the tacks when completed. Carefully ease pattern from loops without tearing paper, then gently separate the material layers, pulling up loops, and cut midway between threads.

*Marking with crayon or chalk (fig 28)*
Fold back the margins of pattern, and lay a ruler with one edge exactly over fold. Mark lines. Fold pattern back more to locate darts, pocket positions and buttonholes, and mark with crayon, as chalk may not be sufficiently accurate. Place pattern on other side of material and repeat.

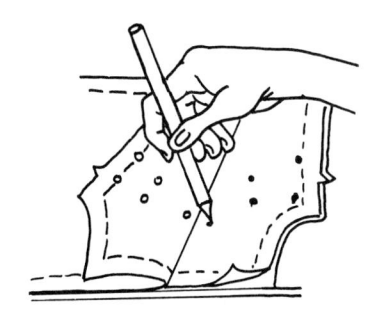

*Fig 28 Marking with crayon*

*Fig 29 Using dressmaking paper and a tracing wheel*

*Dressmaking paper and tracing wheel (fig 29)*
Use this method for crisp, thin materials. The special paper is coated with coloured carbon on one side. Your material must have its wrong side outside if single, inside if double. On single material, place treated side of carbon face down, put pattern over this, and mark indications with tracing wheel, using small crossed lines over dots etc. On double material, place a double layer of carbon paper (treated sides outside) between the layers of fabric, and mark out with tracing wheel, using firm pressure. Always test this procedure on a cutting first.

*Outlining with thread (fig 30)*
For difficult materials (very thin, slippery or thick), where seamlines, pocket positions, grain lines etc need also to be shown on right side, use

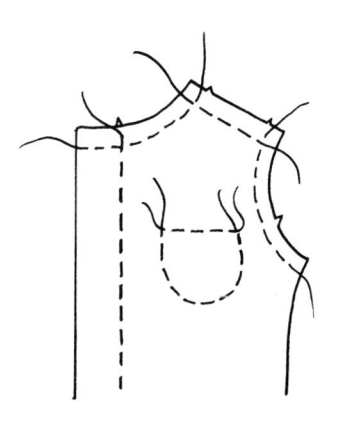

*Fig 30 Outlining with thread*

long tacking stitches to outline. Cross lines at intersections for greater accuracy.

Usually seam lines need not be outlined continuously, but the exact width of turnings should be indicated at regular intervals. Unless you're highly experienced, don't rely on your judgement – a few little miscalculations here and there, and that perfect fit will be in doubt!

*Seams used for children's clothing*
At this stage, decide what seams you will use, and how edges are to be finished. This will depend entirely on the material.

1 For thin cottons, Terylene or Fortrel and lawn, 'linenized' synthetics etc, a *French seam* (*fig 31*) is strong, neat, and prevents fraying.

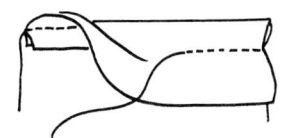

*Fig 31 French seam*

*Fig 32 Zig-zagging and overcasting*

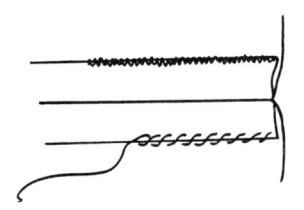

2 Thicker materials and wool mixtures usually have *open seams* with neatened edges. If materials have a firm, close weave, they may be neatened with *zig-zagging* (*fig 32, top*) – but always try this out first. Looser weaves will frill and break out if the zig-zag attachment is used. Then, hand *overcasting* (*fig 32*) is a must.

*Fig 33 Run and fell seam*

3 For blouses, slips, panties, jeans, and dungarees, a *run and fell* (*fig 33*) or *overlaid* seam is best, being strong, flat and comfortable. On stiffer materials the 'fell' is often on the right side, and stitched with contrasting thread as a

decoration, as on jeans, skirts, and safari-type jackets in twill or denim. The edges of closely knit bonded fabrics may sometimes be pinked as a neatening (one of the few instances where this may be satisfactory!).

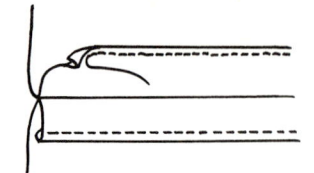

*Fig 34 Edge stitching*

4 A neat finish for cottons, where an open seam is preferred, is fine *edge stitching* (*fig 34*). Here, the raw edges are turned in singly 3 mm ($\frac{1}{8}$ in) and machined before any seams are joined. Zigzagging edges too should be done before assembling the garment. This is a time-saver, and far easier to do at this stage.

5 *Piping* (*fig 35*) will add particular emphasis to a seam. Insert the cord into the crossway strips for binding.

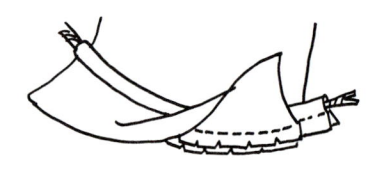

*Fig 35 Piped and corded seam*

**Assembling a garment the logical way**
Modern methods of assembly are based on those used in the factory workroom, and are quicker, easier, but no less accurate than the old laborious methods which involved much preliminary tacking together, and many tedious fittings, especially irksome to children.

The Unit Plan simply means doing all the work necessary on each piece of a garment before joining it to any other piece. The advantages are:

1 Time saved, less handling and stretching of the material.

2 The smaller units are easier to work on, and to manoeuvre under the presser foot – you can see exactly what you're doing.

3 Busy mothers can pick up and work on a single unit without having to spread all the work out each time. Precious odd half hours can be put

to excellent use! Main pattern manufacturers usually plan their instruction sheets along these lines now, anyway.

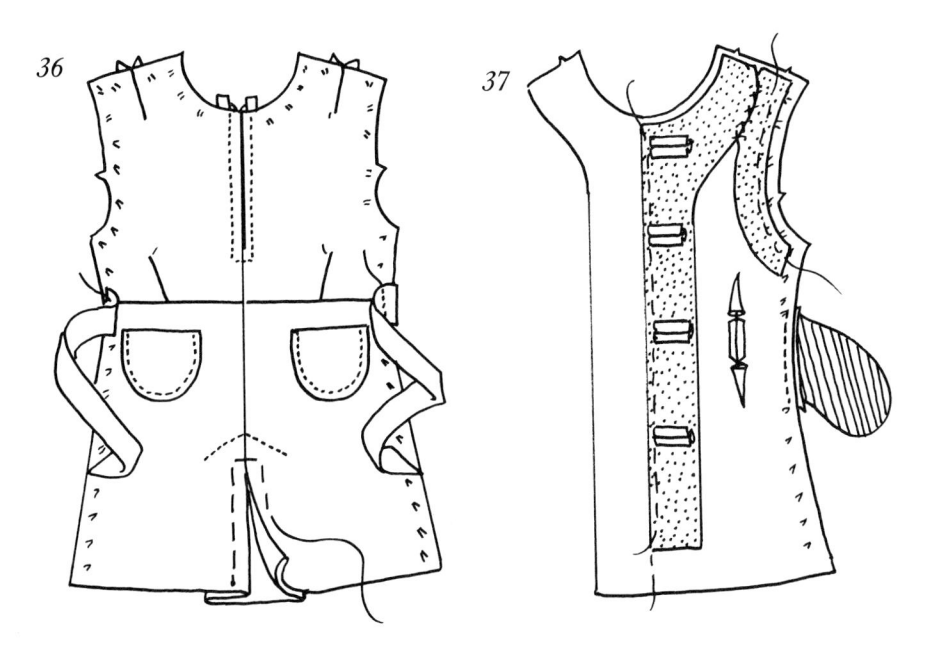

*Fig 36 (above) Dress front before assembly of complete garment*

*Fig 37 (right) Coat front before assembly*

Having previously checked and adjusted all positions of buttonholes, pockets, pleats, darts etc on the pattern, as described (chapter 2), you can confidently complete all the details straight away. It's usually possible to do all the following before putting a garment together (*figs 36, 37, and 38*):

1. Zig-zag edges or otherwise neaten them, including edges of facings.

2. Stitch and press darts (chapter 8).

3. Tack interfacings on fronts, armholes, and necks (where used) and behind pocket positions.

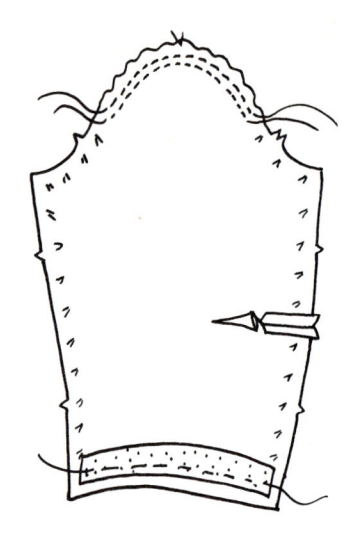

*Fig 38 Sleeve before assembly*

4 Make and apply pockets, except where these cross an intersection, eg astride a panel seam. Where pockets are incorporated in side seams, bag halves are joined to each side seam where indicated (chapter 13).

5 Make bound buttonholes, less facings (chapter 12).

6 Make front or back neck openings.

7 Tack up pleats (chapter 8).

8 It's also far easier to tack back and front bodice pieces to the respective skirt sections before shoulder or side seams are joined.

9 Make sleeve openings (continuous lap, faced, etc) (chapter 12).

10 Prepare sleeve head (chapter 11).

When these operations are completed:

11 Join shoulder seams, and press.

12 Make collar, and press (chapter 10).

13  Apply facings at neck and down fronts, where applicable. Apply collar (chapter 10).

14  Set in one-piece sleeves at top, and tack up underarm and side seams.

15  Complete bound buttonholes.

16  Only now should it be necessary to try the garment on the child. If buttons etc have been sewn on before fitting, the set of collar and sleeve can be checked more accurately.

17  Next, check fit at sides, and mark any slight adjustments with downwards pointing pins.

18  Note hem length, adjusting if necessary.

19  Remove garment, stitch and press side seams, turn up hem (chapter 14), and give the garment a final pressing off.

20  If to be lined, make up lining and put in (chapter 17).

21  Make belt (if any), carriers, and neck hanger (chapter 17).

Tackling dressmaking this way will certainly produce a fresher looking garment with the minimum of worry or bother for yourself or for the young wearers.

# 7
# Pressing is a Priority

Many materials used today for children's clothing need little or no pressing or ironing in wear. But in their making up the time-honoured rule 'press as you sew' still applies. Correct pressing techniques are sure steps to a professional looking garment.

Your iron, ironing board, sleeve board, press cloths – fine muslin, cotton sheeting, and possibly twill for really heavy wool cloth – with a bowl of water and a synthetic sponge, should always be at hand when you dressmake. Press cloths soon look grey and stained from a mixture of not-quite-fast dyes, and should be renewed frequently. Damp-pressing tends to roughen and discolour your iron. Keep its sole-plate smooth and shining by cleaning with a damp cloth, dipped in a non-scratch scouring powder, when the iron has cooled after using.

Press pad and roller, as described in chapter 4, with possibly an unused oven mitt, are also indispensable aids to good pressing. A tiny travelling iron is also useful for darts and getting into nooks and crannies on small garments. A spray atomizer used for pot plants is handy for dampening cotton and synthetics. Don't use a steam iron on synthetics – threads may melt!

An essential precaution before pressing or ironing any part of the garment, is to test a cutting to find out exactly what temperature suits it best. Test for both dry and damp heat, and make sure the latter leaves no watermark.

**General rules to remember when pressing**

1 Pressing isn't ironing! It's an up-and-down movement – never a sliding one.

2 Press with the grain, not across it, especially when pressing (or ironing) on the bias.

3 Most materials are pressed on the wrong side, but pockets, buttonholes and pleats are pressed on the right side over a damp or dry cloth, according to the material.

4 Remove all tackings, and weed out any half concealed stray pins. A wipe with a well squeezed out damp sponge may be enough to dampen some synthetic fabrics.

5 Nowadays, the heat settings on your iron may be misleading, since so many materials are made with yarns of mixed content – natural and synthetic. Each may respond differently to heat. It's only by careful testing that you'll find the right heat setting for each.

**How, where and when to press**

*Seams*
Press each seam before making an intersection. On thicker materials, press plain seams open over

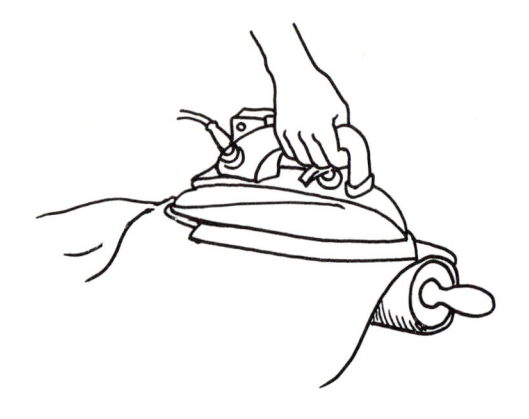

*Fig 39 Using a padded roller*

a padded roller (*fig 39*), or, failing this, a thick magazine covered with a folded tea towel. This will prevent any impression from showing on the right side.

If your machine is an automatic, or has a zig-zag attachment, it's a good idea to neaten edges of main seams before assembling. Iron edges, if they've stretched.

After stitching a plain seam, press the edges together, and then press them open. Place seams absolutely straight on the ironing board. Loss of shape is often caused by careless placing, giving the work that unwelcome home-made look.

Curved seams should lie in a perfect curve. This is easier if they are pressed over the shaped pad. Avoid stretching the material on curves, or anywhere where the line of stitching is on the bias. If necessary, pin shaped seams into place, removing pins as you reach them.

French seams should be thin and crisp. After stitching the first row, press the wider edge over the trimmed one. Then stitch the second row, and press again. Run and fell seams are pressed after the first row, edge folded and stitched, and pressed again.

*Darts*
These are intended to shape the material to fit over curved parts of the body, so it's essential to press these over a shaped pad, or a rolled up tea towel, instead of spoiling their shape on a flat board, as often happens! On thick materials, slit dart halfway down, trim seam edges, and press point into a small central pleat. Darts should be pressed towards – but not quite up to – the point. Press shoulder darts towards armhole, waist darts towards sides, and elbow darts downwards.

*Gathers*
These can be spoiled by flattening the tops near their join to plain material. Lift the ungathered material with one hand, while holding the fullness out taut with the iron. Move the point gently up between the folds as far as possible. A tiny iron is useful here.

*Set-in sleeves*
If you have one, use a sleeve board. Otherwise, put the sleeve wrong side outside over the padded roller to press the underarm seam. Press the sleeve head over the shaped pad, as described in chapter 11. Never iron or press the lower half of an armhole seam, as this will stretch the line out of shape.

*Pressing special seams*
Seams at a junction may pose a problem. The rule, however, is simple. First press the straightest seam, then the more curved one over it, eg at leg and body intersections of jeans etc do the leg seams first, then open and press the front-to-back seam over them.

Top-stitched seams are pressed first to flatten

the 'ridge', then top-stitched and pressed again –
usually on right side, over a cloth.

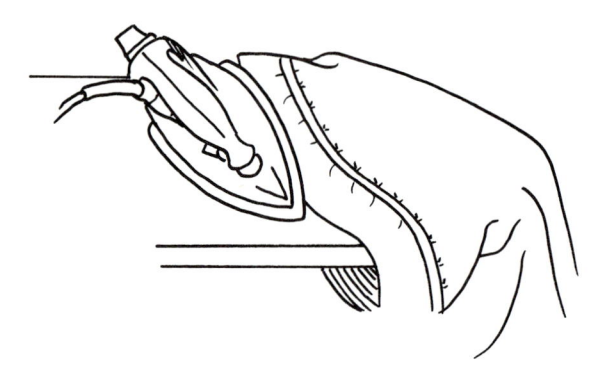

*Fig 40 Pressing hem edge*

*Hems*
Press turned-in or bound edges before hem is
turned up. Place curved hems on the board in
sections, following the curved shape. Be very
careful not to stretch the material in doing so.
Press all hems on the very edge only, using the
side of the iron (*fig 40*). Pressing the full width of
turn-up makes an ugly ridge on the right side.

*Pockets, belts, pleats and buttonholes*
These are pressed over a cloth on the right side.
Pleats – contrary to usual practice – should have
their tackings left in for a light first pressing.
Then remove tacks by clipping at frequent intervals (don't pull out long lengths) and press again,
more firmly. Support pressed pleats over a chair,
and hold them in with hair grips.

**Pressing special materials**

*Pure wool*
Must be pre-shrunk. Otherwise it will shrink
unevenly when individual parts are pressed during making up. People often imagine that dry

cleaning can't shrink materials. But this can certainly happen unless woollens are pre-shrunk. Lay the folded material on a padded table, and cover with a wrung out cloth of same width. Using an up-and-down movement only, go over entire length with a hot iron. Reverse material to do other side. Allow to dry before handling. Alternatively, roll material in a damp sheet, and leave overnight. Press off lightly.

*Jersey*
Pressed on wrong side, always following main ribs – never across them. Be careful not to pull or stretch fabric.

*Pile fabrics*
These need little pressing – merely on the seams. If very thick, first trim back pile from inside turnings to reduce bulk. Lay extra padding over board, and press seams apart. If turnings won't lie flat, smear a *thin* film of Copydex underneath and press them down. Brush up the pile immediately. Modern, synthetic velvets are popular for children's 'best' dresses, skirts, boys' jackets, and long pants. Here, too, only the seams need pressing during making up. Press on wrong side over well padded roller, using slightly dampened cloth, and tip only of iron. Test out first. Don't handle until dry.

*Corduroy*
This will take a more thorough but light pressing over padded board. Press on wrong side only. Brush pile the way it runs.

# 8
# Dealing with Darts, Pleats, Gathers etc

A working knowledge of the different methods of controlling fullness is particularly important when making children's clothes. Allowing plenty of room for ease and growth is the first essential. But fullness should be offset by fit, eg a full smock, blouse, or skirt is controlled by a well-fitting yoke, band, or bodice. It's the contrast that looks so attractive.

Gathering, smocking, ruching, tucking, elasticating, and drawing up fullness by slotted ribbon or elastic are decorative ways of controlling fullness. Less conspicuous methods include easing and shrinking, also darting (to reduce small amounts of fullness to give fit). Pleating is another excellent method of controlling fullness while adding very little bulk. The method chosen will depend on the material, the garment, and also the child's age.

Here are some tried and tested methods of tackling the various techniques.

**Gathering** (*fig 41*)
Always popular for children's dresses, full sleeves, frills, and ruffles. Suitable for fine and lightweight fabrics. Allow two to three times the

*Fig 41 Gathering skirt on to bodice*

finished width – the finer the material, the more you should allow. When short of material, one or two gathered sections will look more effective than a larger area skimped. To hang properly, gathers must fall along the lengthwise – never the crosswise – threads of the material.

Machine gathering is quick and satisfactory. Set your machine at its longest stitch, and loosen the tension. See that at least 10 cm (4 in) of thread projects from the reel and bobbin. For large areas, use buttonhole thread in the bobbin only. Working on the right side, do the first row just within the fitting line. (This saves the bother of pulling out gathering threads later.) Do the second row 6 mm ($\frac{1}{4}$ in) above the first, leaving spare thread at ends. Divide the edge to be gathered, and the plain edge into equal sections. Mark with pins put in at right angles. Draw up to fit, from *both* ends. Wind ends of thread around pins at each end, and arrange gathers evenly before pinning each section to the corresponding pins on plain edge. Tack the two edges together (right sides facing) and machine on the gathered side, smoothing to prevent gathers from catching in machine needle. For double yokes, place gathered edge between facing and yoke *after* doing first row of machining and machine exactly over this to ensure accuracy. Turnings are pressed towards plain side.

Automatic machine gathering is also satisfactory, provided trials are made first to find exactly how much material is taken up per 2·5 cm (1 in).

When doing hand gathering, measure each length of thread to be used, allowing extra at each end. For large areas, divide the edge into sections, and use double thread to prevent risk of thread snapping when pulling up.

**Smocking** (*figs 42a and b*)
A traditional and ever-popular method of controlling fullness on children's dresses, blouses, smocks etc. The best effects are obtained by using one or two contrasting threads. Always allow three or four times the finished width for smocking. Material mustn't be skimped or the effect will be spoiled.

To form smocking, designs are built up from two or three simple stitches. Each stitch is taken up from a pre-marked dot. You can mark out dots yourself, by following a pulled crosswise thread, with spacings accurately marked. Or you can buy sheets of dots, to transfer on to material, from most needlework suppliers. Gingham is ideal for smocking, since you can dispense with marking, using the checks as a guide, taking up two threads at each corner of checks. Here are the two main stitches. They may be combined to form many different designs.

*Fig 42a Smocking – rope or cable stitch*

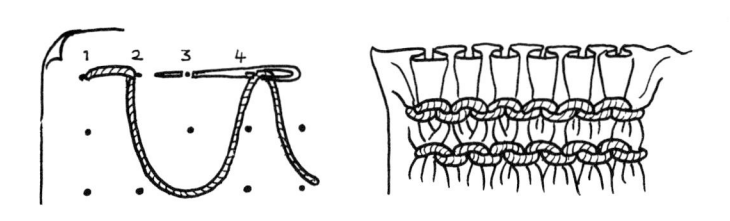

*Rope or cable (fig 42a)*
Using two to six strands of embroidery silk or cotton, secure threads behind first dot, and bring needle out, point towards left. Working from left to right, take up second dot keeping thread *below* needle. Pull thread up taut, take up third dot, keeping thread *above* needle. Proceed to fourth dot, with thread *below* needle, and on to dots five, six etc, keeping thread above and below alternately to end of row. Work all rows from left to right.

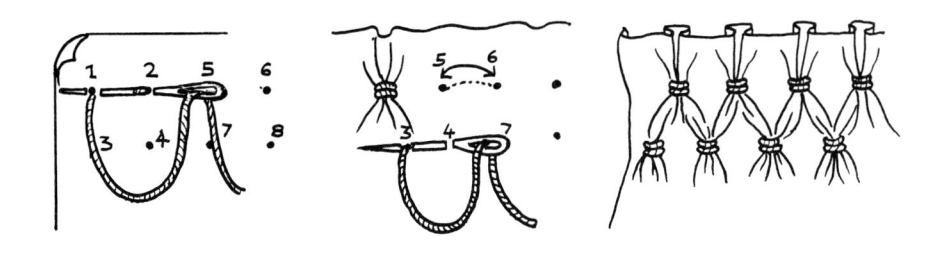

*Fig 42b Smocking – honeycomb stitch*

*Honeycomb stitch (fig 42b)*
Starting on left, bring needle out at first dot, with thread *below*, catch up second dot, take up first dot again, and pull thread taut. Take needle down to third dot inside material. Bring needle out, and take up fourth dot, return to third dot, and pull up thread. Proceed to fifth and sixth dots etc. Complete all rows similarly. Thread is kept below needle throughout.

**Shirring** (*fig 43*)

This consists of any number of gathered rows forming a deep section of controlled fullness. Allowances of material will depend on type and thickness used. The finer this is, the more you'll require, but never less than twice the finished measurement for fine materials, and one and a half times for thicker materials.

Working on right side, with loosened tension on under thread, stitch required number of rows. Average distance between rows is 6 mm ($\frac{1}{4}$ in) – 1·2 cm ($\frac{1}{2}$ in). When rows are completed, draw up under threads evenly, and fasten off strongly. Stroke gathers downwards. Back the shirred portion with lining to give support.

**Elasticating**

This is worked in the same way, using elastic thread in the bobbin. This method needs no support on the inside.

**Ribbon in slot** (*fig 44*)

Used at the waist and at ends of full sleeves of girls' dresses. The fullness can be flattened out for easy ironing. Apply a band of self material of width required, behind area to be drawn up. Make bound or worked buttonholes for ribbons to emerge on to right side before applying band.

**Tucks** (*fig 45*)

Another useful and decorative alternative. They can be any width from 3 mm ($\frac{1}{8}$ in) – 1·5 cm ($\frac{5}{8}$ in) or more, sometimes taken right across a bodice, or arranged in groups of uneven numbers (odd numbers are considered easier on the eye than even numbers!). Distances between tucks is a matter of choice. If tucks are arranged so that

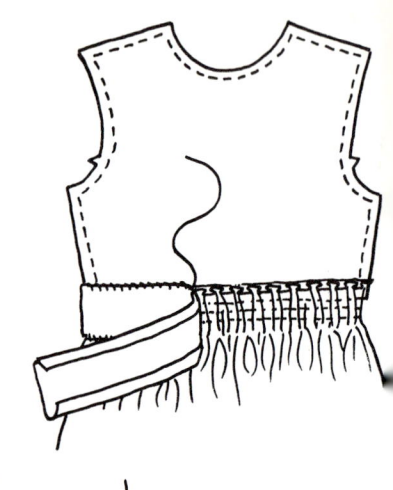

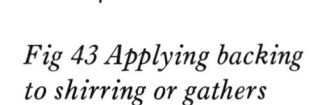

*Fig 43 Applying backing to shirring or gathers*

*Fig 44 Using a ribbon in a slot*

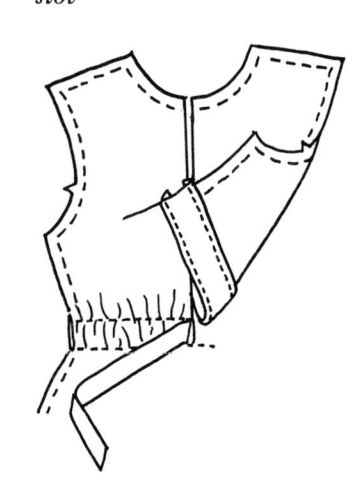

*Fig 45 Tucks used decoratively*

*Fig 46 A card is useful for marking tucks*

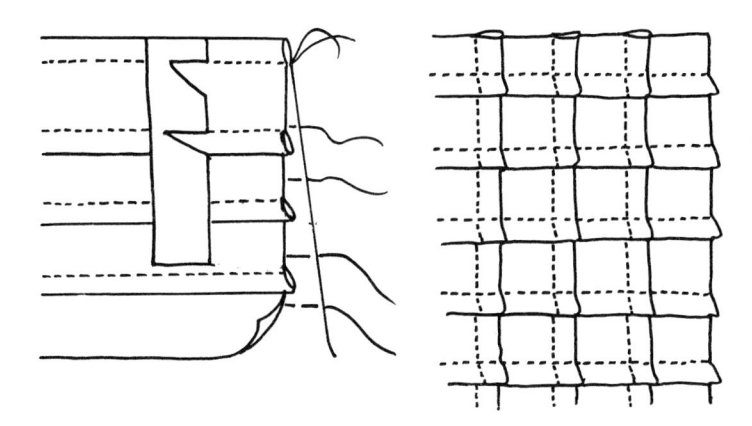

the fold of each tuck meets the stitching of the next, three times the amount of material is needed. Each individual tuck takes up twice its width. Horizontal tucks around the hem of a child's dress are a useful method of providing for growth.

Preliminary marking and/or tacking is essential. Get one tuck off-grain and the whole lot will be wrong! A square weave is best, as you can follow the threads more easily. Where practicable, pull up a thread where the fold of each tuck will be. Otherwise, tack exactly along a thread. A notched cardboard marker (*fig 46*) helps in spacing. Fold and crease each tuck, and use a fine stitch. When tucks are completed, pull top threads to wrong side, and fasten ends off with a needle through both threads. Press tucks away from centre front.

### Darts

An indispensable dressmaking technique for reducing fullness to give shape. They are used:

1 On skirts from waist to hip at back and front, also on trousers.

2 On sleeves, from elbow to wrist, and horizontally from elbow.

3 Across the chest from underarm.

4 At the back of shoulder and/or neck.

Darts are normally made on wrong side of material, tapering off just before the point where ease is required, eg at shoulders, elbow point, and bust point on older girls. There are three kinds of darts: from a seam; double-ended, used at the waist of one-piece dresses; dart tucks – a cross between a dart and a tuck, used at the waist of little dresses, from the shoulders of blouses, etc.

1 To make *darts from a seam*, fold material exactly where marked. Stitch from the widest part, narrowing off to a mere thread's breadth at 6 mm ($\frac{1}{4}$ in) from the point – the secret of preventing that too-familiar 'poke' (*figs 47a and b*)!

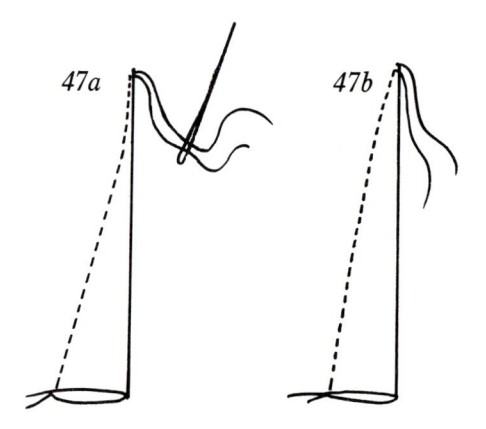

*Fig 47a Right way to make a dart*

*Fig 47b Wrong way to make a dart*

2 For a *double-ended dart* (*figs 48a and b*), start near the centre of fold, and stitch to one end, as above. Start again near centre, overlapping stitching by 2·5 cm (1 in), and machine to the other end. Don't tie off ends of darts, but bring top thread through to inside, thread both into a needle and oversew. Notch edges.

*Figs 48a and b Double-ended darts*

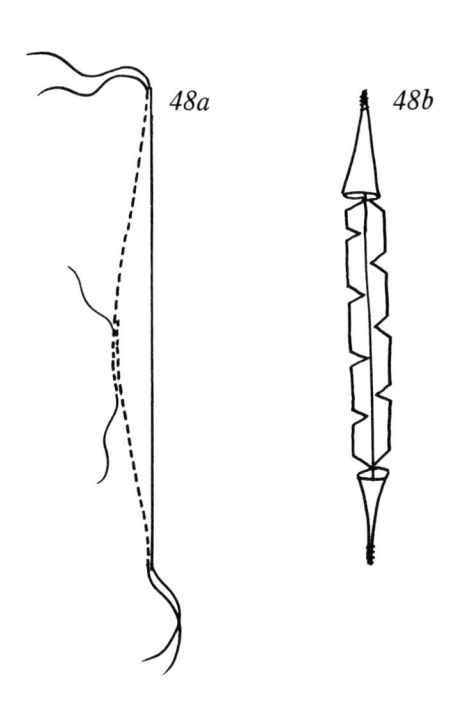

*Figs 49a and b Dart tucks*

*Fig 50 Dart opened and pressed*

3  For *dart tucks* (*figs 49a and b*), fold material exactly on grain, and stitch from centre of fold to one end, turn and stitch to other end. Turn, and go back to centre, overlapping stitching a little way. This prevents loose stitches showing at ends.

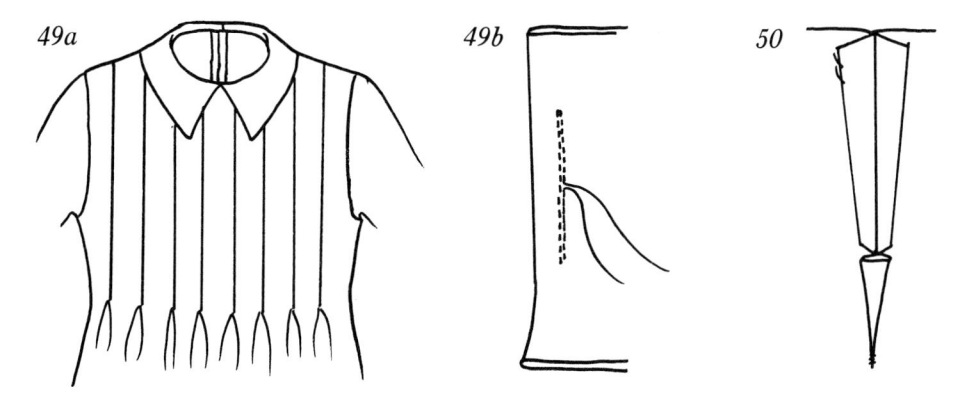

**Pleats**

The least bulky way of enclosing a great deal of material while allowing maximum freedom below, eg a fully pleated skirt or tunic. Pleats can be enclosed in panel seams, and are also used in the backs of school coats, and on boys' and girls' shirts.

Types of pleats:

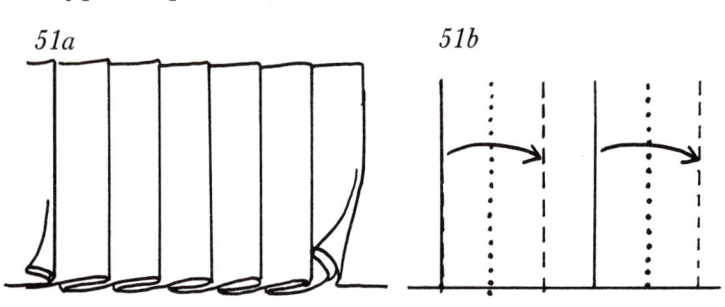

*Figs 51a and b Knife pleats*

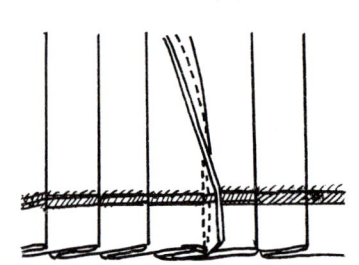

*Fig 52 Arranging join in pleats*

1 *Knife pleats* (*figs 51a and b*). All pleats go in the same direction, usually with no space between them, and each upper fold meets each under fold.

2 *Box pleats* (*fig 53*) are formed by two equal pleats, each turned in the opposite direction.

3 *Inverted pleats* (*fig 54*) are the exact opposite; the folds meet in front, forming a box pleat on the inside.

4 *Pleat incorporated in panel seam*, with (*fig 55*) or without backing piece.

5 *Accordion pleats* – lots of tiny box pleats, covering an entire skirt.

6 *Sunray* or graduated pleats (narrow at the top, gradually widening towards the hem) are unsuitable for attempting at home. Special industrial heat-setting equipment is required to produce these.

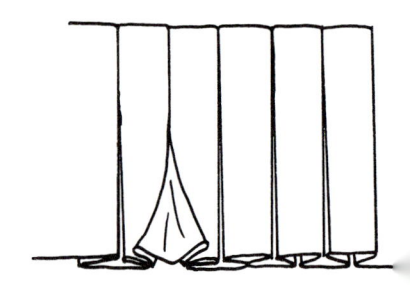

*Fig 53 Box pleats*

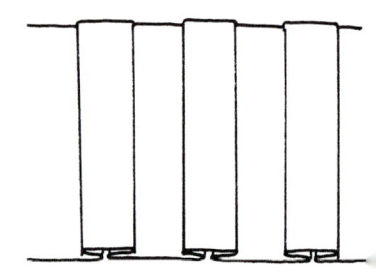

*Fig 54 Inverted pleats*

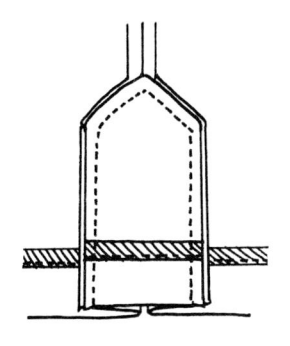

*Fig 55 Backed pleat*

For each pleat, allow three times its width, eg a 5 cm (2 in) pleat takes 15 cm (6 in) of material, The spacing between is a matter of choice. Where pleats meet, whatever their size, the same proportion of material will be needed to produce a certain finished measurement, eg twelve 5 cm (2 in) pleats will equal six 10 cm (4 in) pleats etc.

Accurate preliminary marking is essential. This must be on the straight grain, using different colours for tacking or marking (on wrong side). Use one colour for fold line, and another for placement line where each fold rests.

Plan pleats so that seams come on inside of folds, and join and press seams before making pleats. A side opening should come inside a pleat, leaving seam open by amount required.

For children's fully pleated skirts, complete hem before joining side seams. The turnings are neatened at bottom of seams by clipping turnings up diagonally and oversewing. Begin stitching side seams at hem edge for accuracy.

First make sure the length is correct. It's best here to stitch skirt to a double waistband which can be let down later instead of the hem.

At waist edge of skirts, machine pleats, when placed and tacked, on fitting line, 7·5 cm (3 in) down.

To place pleats, crease each one on its outside fold, and bring this to meet the corresponding placement fold, pinning as you go. Then tack each pleat all the way down, remove pins and press from inside *and* outside over a cloth, with heat setting according to material (see chapter 7).

# 9
# The Importance of Interfacing

Choosing the right interfacing, and using it correctly, is just as important when you're making a toddler's winter coat or a child's blazer as when making a tailored coat or blazer for an adult. The modern child's clothing should be equally well tailored and professional looking in every detail. Well set-in collars, flat non-curling lapels, crisp pockets and front edges will depend largely on the interfacing and its application.

There's a right interfacing for every dressmaking and tailoring job. In fact, there are more than sixty varieties on the market, though most shops may only stock a few of these. So shop around, and don't be put off with one that isn't quite suitable for the particular material you're going to use.

**Types of interfacing**
Interfacings fall into two broad categories – woven and non-woven. Woven types are just that – woven on a loom, with lengthwise and crosswise threads, in a plain or twill weave. These are available in many weights and qualities, made from cotton, rayon, and synthetic fibres. The finest are fine net and organdie, while the heaviest

are thick cotton and synthetic horsehair. In between these is a whole range of cotton and linen-like interfacings.

Non-woven interfacings are basically different in construction, and not necessarily suitable for every job – though many people think they are! They are made of various fibres of different origins, pressed into solid sheets. They are all very light and have no 'grain' or directional weave to consider. There is no stretch or give in them, so the non-fraying edges can be safely trimmed close to stitching. Non-woven interfacings are also porous and unshrinkable. Odd pieces may be joined and matched merely by laying one edge over another, held with a single row of stitching, which certainly makes for economy. There are several makes, one of which comes packaged in neat rolls. measuring approximately 1 metre × 50 cm (1 × ½ yd). Various qualities are packaged this way, including non-iron and iron-on types together with suggestions as to the special uses of each. Bondina is a fusible interfacing, packaged in narrow widths, used mainly for hems and small areas. The adhesive melts under heat, bonding two layers of material together.

### Where to use interfacing, and what to use where

Interfacing is incorporated into a garment wherever extra stiffness or support is needed, eg in collars, pockets, belts, cuffs, pleats, down fronts, or where extra strain may occur. The choice will depend on the particular job in hand. Sometimes, more than one type or weight of interfacing may be advisable in the same garment. It's better to choose an interfacing slightly lighter in weight than the material – never use one that is heavier. It's easy to spoil a garment by making too solid fronts and a board-like collar out of keeping with the material used. The heavy interfacings of the canvas/horsehair types are generally unsuitable for children's clothing. For general dressmaking purposes, light to medium weight qualities of both woven and non-woven types are the ones you'll need. When using fine, sheer materials, as for little girls' party dresses, an interfacing is likely to show through as a shadow. Here, it's better to use fine net or muslin, or a double thickness of self material in plackets, cuffs, collars, or sashes. Use the same to support buttons and between facings.

Always choose light coloured interfacings for use with pale shades, whatever the material, and black, grey, or brown interfacing for dark colours, eg school coats, blazers, and trousers etc. Light facings can show under dark colours, except on really heavy cloth. Sometimes, confusion arises between the meaning and purpose of *interfacing* and *interlining*. The former is generally used only for stiffening and supporting small areas, eg down fronts, in collars, cuffs, and belts etc (*figs 56, 57, and 58*), whereas interlining is often used to back larger areas, and sometimes an entire garment, to give extra body, and to hold the garment's shape.

Avoid using non-woven interfacing on knitted materials. Because these are stretchy, they will look bubbly and uneven where they are interfaced with rigid material. Knitted fabrics should be interfaced with woven material, applied rather loosely to allow some give. Always use woven interfacing for roll-over collars and revers, because these must be moulded to fit – an impos-

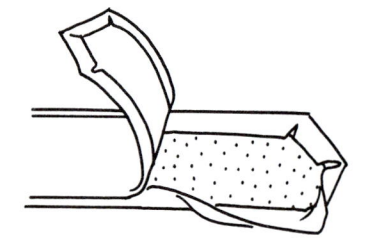

*Fig 56 Interfacing a belt*

*Fig 57 Interfacing a pleat*

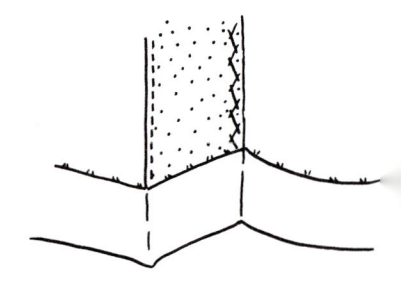

*Fig 58 Interfacing pockets*

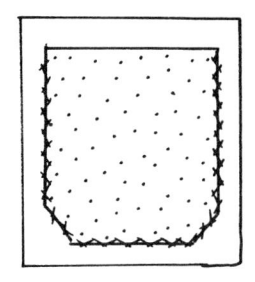

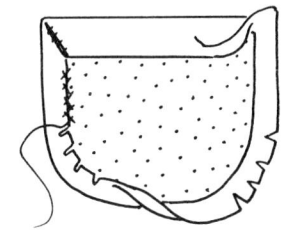

sibility with non-woven interfacings, which would crinkle and pull – an effect one sees all too often! Another pitfall is the possible shrinking of woven interfacings when the garment is washed, and even after dry cleaning. Unless this type is marked 'pre-shrunk' it's wise to soak the interfacing in cold water for an hour before use. Don't rub or twist it, but allow it to drip dry. When almost dry, lay interfacing flat on a padded table or board, and iron along the lengthwise threads only, to avoid displacing the weave.

Interfacing is applied to the fronts of coats and jackets; behind pocket positions, pleats, and other places where strengthening is needed; and on collars and cuffs before you start to assemble the garment. Where no separate pattern is given for a front interfacing, cut one from garment front pattern, following the shape of neck and straight down to the hemline, but without turn-up allowance. Cut interfacing 5 cm (2 in) wide along shoulder line. Cut a back neck interfacing pattern 5 cm (2 in) wide from back of garment. Some little coats and jackets have a deep, curved interfacing at the back. This holds the whole back shoulder area in a good shape, and adds extra warmth. Cut this from the back pattern. (See chapter 17.)

On thicker interfacings, as used in school coats and boys' jackets, trim quite close to the

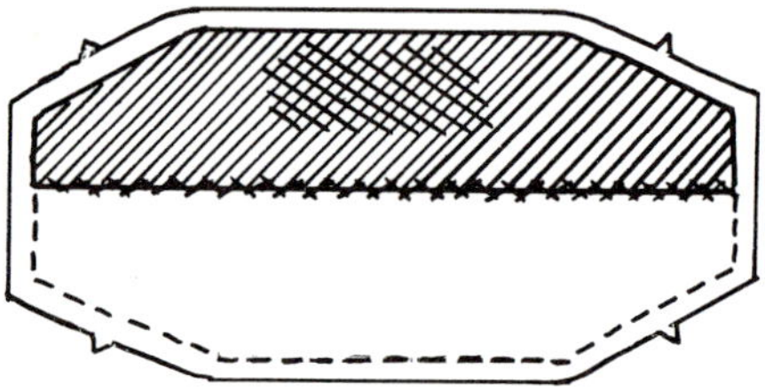

*Figs 59a and b How to interface a collar*

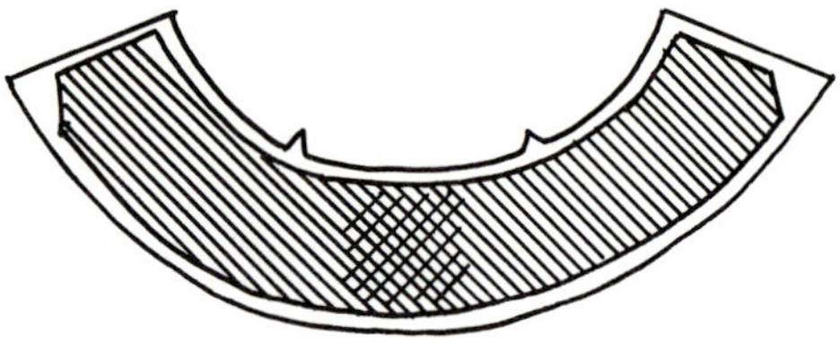

stitching line and catch stitch interfacing edge to the cloth turnings. This will prevent any ridges from showing on the finished edges. Do the same with pocket flaps and collars.

The interfacing of collars (*figs 59a and b*) needs special care to obtain that crisp, tailored look. On any collar that rolls over, use woven interfacing, cut on the true cross. After stitching, edges should be layered, and outside curves notched – inside ones clipped – on alternate edges. This way, you can clip nearer to stitching. At corners, slash turnings close to stitching, sloping up gradually.

Unlike non-woven interfacings, which can be laid on the pattern in any direction, woven kinds must be laid and cut on *exactly* the same grain as the material – the slightest deviation will spoil the 'set' of the affected part.

Where darts come into an interfaced area (*figs 60a and b*), cut the interfacing away close to the stitched dart. If darts are slashed and opened, herringbone the edges into place over the interfacing. Stitches mustn't go through to right side. (See chapter 17 for tailored darts.)

*Figs 60a and b How to treat darts in interfacing*

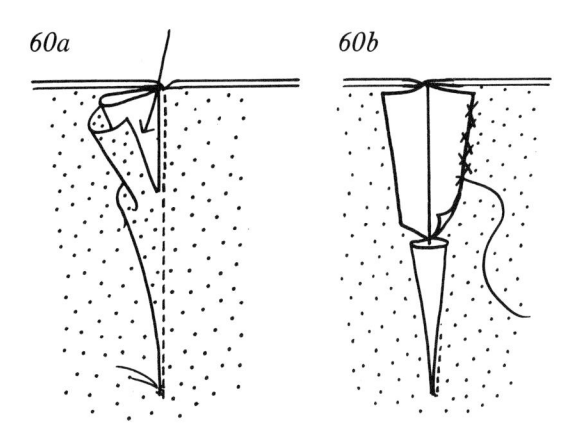

60a   60b

Hems on heavier material look smoother and hang better, with no visible ridge, if hem is turned up on to a strip of interfacing about 2 cm (¾ in) wider than turn-ups. (See chapter 17.) Non-woven interfacing is also used to strengthen ends of openings and plackets.

**Hints on using iron-on interfacings**
Whether using woven or non-woven interfacings of the iron-on kind, make sure your material will stand up to the temperature necessary to melt the adhesive, as this varies considerably. Some are suitable for linens, wool and heavier cottons, and melt at a high temperature; others, intended for use with synthetic materials, have a suitably low melting point. Look out for this information on the ready-packaged kind. If bought off the roll, you'll have to experiment. It's the safest policy, anyway.

# 10
# Collars with Style

Whether well-fitting and tailored, or light and frilly, a collar always adds interest and style to a garment. But nowhere are faults more noticeable! We see lopsided points and thick, knobbly ones, hard, ridgy edges, bubbly unequal fullness at collar sides, undercollars too full, and seam edges showing instead of rolling underneath. Yet all these disasters are easy to avoid if the right precautions are taken. Precision and accuracy are the keynotes in collar making – measuring and checking at every stage.

Basically, collars fall into one of two categories – those that lie almost flat over the shoulders, eg Peter Pan, shawl and sailor types, and those which are cut straighter, causing the collar to rise and roll over at the sides and back. Exceptions are the mandarin, bow tie and straight stand-up styles, having little or no shaping. Here are some basic hints for achieving perfect collars of all kinds:

1 Ensure that the neckline of the garment fits the child correctly. Collars are made to fit the

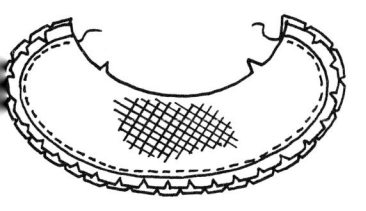

*Fig 61 Woven interfacing in a collar*

*Fig 62 Peter Pan collar*

*Fig 63a (below) Making a pattern for a Peter Pan collar*

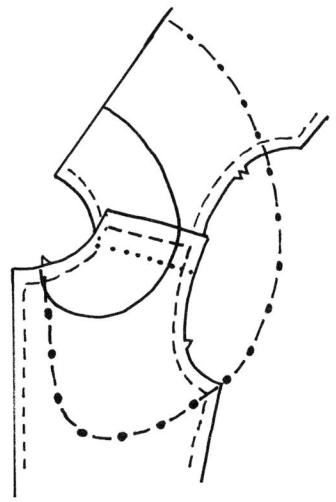

garment – not the reverse. And a collar should always be made slightly tighter than the neckline it's fitted to – never eased on to it. Always test the collar against the neckline, and note the difference. If collar is too large, or too small, adjust it so that collar edge measures 2–2·5 cm ($\frac{3}{4}$–1 in) less than neckline between end notches. Always fold the collar in half to test it; sometimes one pointed (or curved) end gets stretched during the actual making.

2 Collars are usually made double, and when folded over in the correct 'roll', the upper layer will be slightly shorter than the under layer. Pin in this position and trim edges level immediately.

3 Apart from those in lace or organdie etc, most collars are improved by a suitable interfacing (see chapter 9) (*fig 61*).

4 When pinning collar to neckline, start by matching centre backs, then notches at either end, putting pins in at right angles. Make sure that the amount of ease mentioned above is divided equally between both sides of neckline. If correct, oversew each end of collar at balance mark to hold in exactly correct place.

*Peter Pan collar (fig 62)*

The most popular type for young children. These collars can be added to most garments with a round close-fitting neckline. To make a pattern (*fig 63a*), place back and front patterns of garment on a plain piece of paper, with seam lines meeting at shoulders. Draw in collar outline to desired shape, and cut out. Cut collar in double material, and interface suitably. Place layers right sides together, stitch, trim, and notch edges.

Turn to right side and press. To attach collar (*fig 63b*) finish front opening, and pin centre back of collar to centre back of garment, underside of collar to right side of garment, matching ends to tacks at fronts. Place and pin a crossway strip 3·8 cm (1½ in) wide along collar edges, keeping all edges level, with ends of crossway strip extending to edges of opening. Tack and stitch on fitting lines. Trim, layer, and clip edges, and turn strip to inside. Turn in free edge, and catch to machine stitches, neatening ends. The finished, fitted collar is shown in *fig 63c*.

Where the opening is at the back, collars are cut in two halves. To ensure that halves meet in centre front, place both together and oversew edges for 6 mm (¼ in) at neck, and attach as one piece.

Little dresses often have a double yoke, with Peter Pan type collar set between layers, as in *figs 64a, b, and c*. Make up and lay the collar piece(s) to neckline on right side of yoke. Place yoke lining over, right side down, tack and stitch through all thicknesses. Clip turnings alternately, and turn to right side.

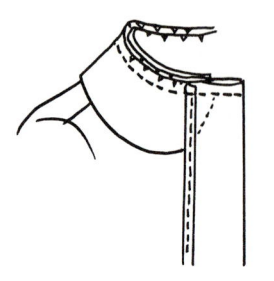

*Fig 63b (above) Attaching a collar*

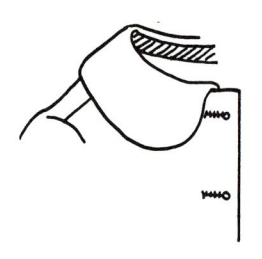

*Fig 63c (above) Finished collar*

*Fig 64a Preparing a Peter Pan collar with a double yoke*

*Fig 64b Layers stitched with collar between*

*Fig 64c Finished collar on yoke*

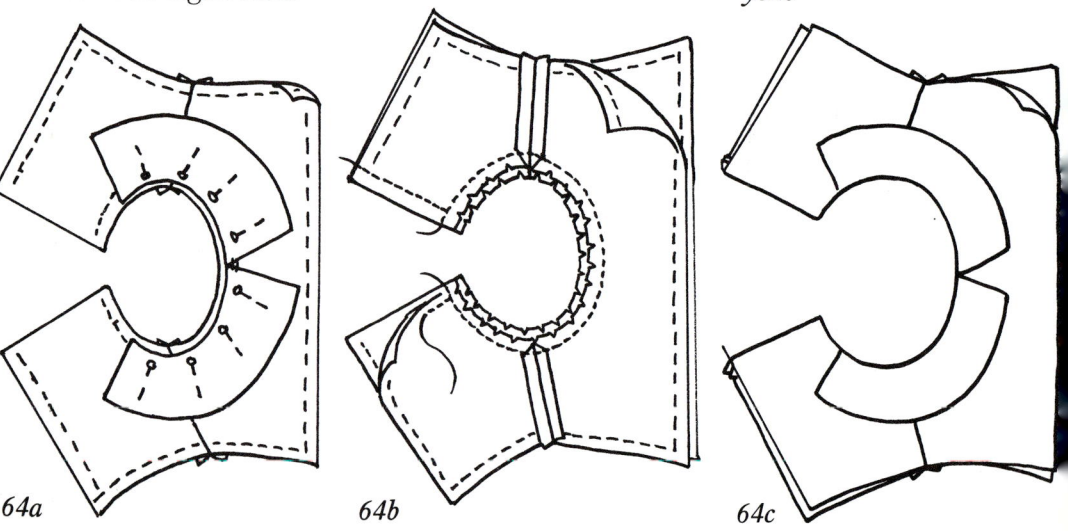

64a   64b   64c

Fig 65 Collar with rise at back

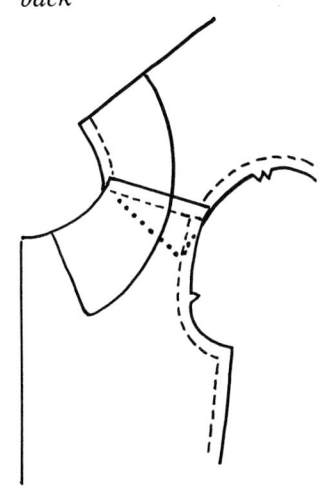

Fig 66 Making a pattern for a collar with a rising back

Figs 67a and b How to interface a stand-up collar

Fig 67c Neatening a stand-up collar (wrong side)

Fig 67d Finished a stand-up collar

*Collar with rise at back (fig 65)*
Place pattern (*fig 66*) of back and front together at shoulders, but overlap shoulder seamlines at armhole end by 1·3–2·5 cm ($\frac{1}{2}$–1 in) according to amount of rise required. Draw outline of collar as for Peter Pan, and try out. The larger the overlap, the higher the rise, of course. Make collar as for Peter Pan, and place to right side of neckline, checking at centre back measurements to each end. Apply crossway binding along seamline, as for Peter Pan.

*A straight collar (stand-up, or turn-down) (figs 67a, b, c, and d)*
Specially suitable for knitted materials. Cut collar from straight piece, twice finished width, plus turnings, for stand-up collar; four times finished width, plus turnings, if it is to turn down. Place and tack cross-cut woven interfacing on inside of half its width, catch stitching inside edge to collar fold line. Fold in half lengthwise, wrong sides out, and stitch ends. Turn to right side, and press. Pin inner side of collar to neckline, matching notches and stitch. Press turnings open, layer them, then press them upwards. Turn free edge inside, and hem to machining. If in woven material, this collar must be cut on the cross.

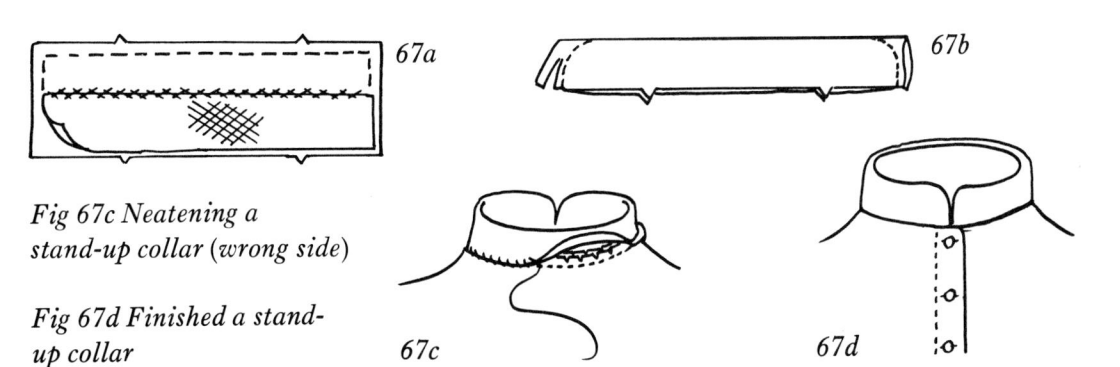

*Fancy collars*
A dainty lace-trimmed or frilled collar will make a plain little dress pretty enough for a party. It is a good idea to make several of these in different materials and with varied trimmings – perhaps with matching cuffs. Draw out the collar shapes, using pattern of front and back, as described. On sheer materials, the collar may be single, if lace-trimmed. In all instances, bind the neck edge with crossway or self binding, and neaten ends. Attach to garment with fine press-studs. On thicker materials, 2·5 cm (1 in) squares of Velcro sewn at either end of collar and garment neck, and at centre back (under neckline edge), may be used to hold in place. Smooth half of Velcro is sewn to garment.

# 11
# Setting in Sleeves Professionally

Most of us have experienced the extreme discomfort of a tight armhole at some time in our lives. When making children's clothes, it is vital to ensure that sleeves are really easy fitting, with plenty of room for growth, especially with tailored coats or jackets in woven material, and dresses and blouses with long sleeves set into cuffs. Yet comfort is often sacrificed for an apparently good fit.

**Types of sleeve**
Basically, there are three kinds of sleeve, each with variations:

1 The traditional set-in sleeve.

2 The raglan type.

3 The magyar (or kimono) style.

There are tricks worth knowing when dealing with all three.

*Plain set-in sleeve*
Difficulties can arise here, because one is actually attempting to mould and fit flat material to a rounded shape of a smaller circumference –

and to compress it invisibly. No wonder results aren't always perfect! The first essential is to measure round seam lines and armhole. The difference should be no more than 5 cm (2 in). If it is more, scoop a little from bottom of armhole – never from the sleeve head. The remaining surplus is disposed of by gathering, easing and/or shrinking. Next, using a large stitch, run two gathering threads between notches on sleeve top; one on fitting line, the other 6 mm ($\frac{1}{4}$ in) above it (*fig 68a*). Draw the threads up to fit notches on armhole, with centre mark at sleeve top coinciding with shoulder seam. Pin remainder to armhole seams (*fig 68b*). Now, holding the gathered top in a convex curve, wrong side uppermost, tack along lower gathering thread, flattening fullness evenly, and backstitching to hold gathered part firmly. Machine fractionally below fitting line, and again just above it. Press turnings together towards sleeve over a shaped pad, and neaten.

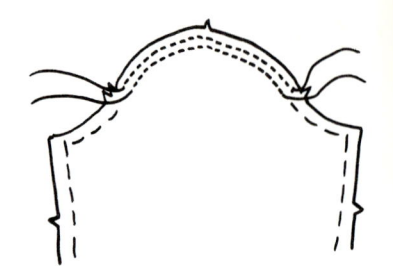

*Fig 68a Where to gather sleeve top*

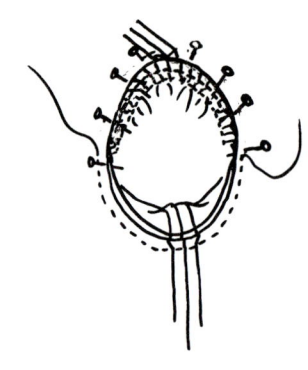

*Fig 68b Pinning sleeve in armhole*

Prepare all-wool materials as described, but place the gathered top over shaped pad, cover with a damp cloth on right side, and dab with a hot iron. Lift cloth, move gathers along slightly, and repeat. The fullness should disappear like snow in the sunshine! But wool/synthetic mixtures won't shrink. Careful manipulation is the answer here.

*Fig 69 Shirt sleeve top stitched*

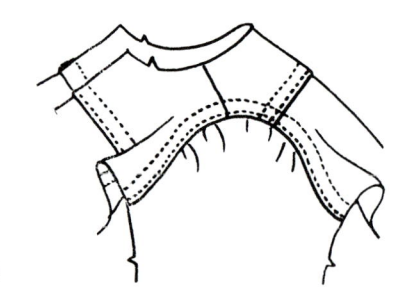

With all lightweight materials, the side seams may be left open until sleeves have been put in, making the job much easier, especially with boys' shirts, pyjamas etc where a run and fell seam is made on the right side (*fig 69*). But for tailored coats and jackets, with a one- or two-piece sleeve, side seams are stitched and pressed before inserting the sleeves, because here

*Fig 70a Sleeve set too far back*

*Fig 70b Sleeve set too far forward*

*Fig 70c Sleeve hanging correctly*

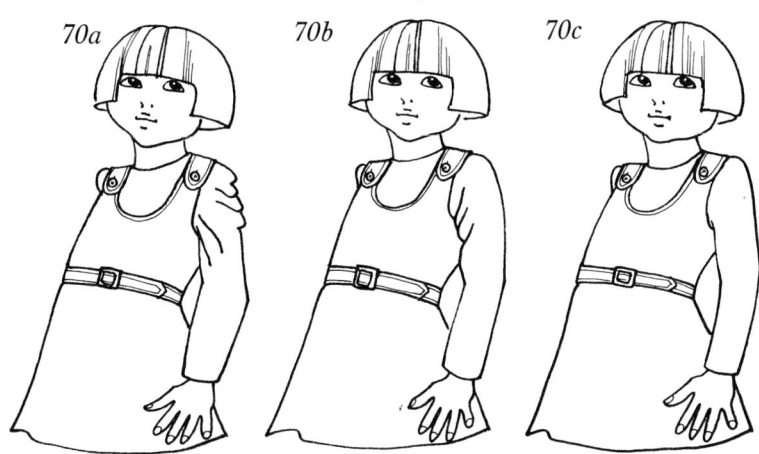

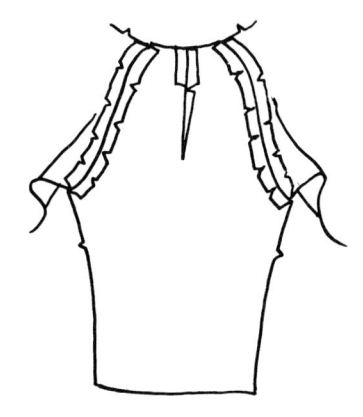

*Fig 71a Raglan sleeve (inside)*

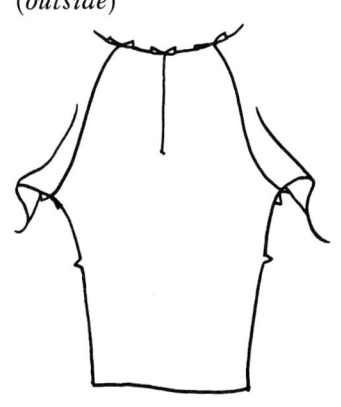

*Fig 71b Raglan sleeve (outside)*

the hang of the sleeve must conform exactly to the natural angle of the individual child's arm. This varies considerably. Prepare sleeve head as above, and stitch and press sleeve seams. Try garment on, and pin the sleeve at the shoulder and underarm only. It should hang smoothly, without wrinkles, and with straight threads running from centre top of shoulder to behind the little finger (*figs 70a, b, and c*). If wrinkles appear either in front or behind top of shoulder, un-pin sleeve and move it slightly towards the back or front until all creases disappear. Re-pin in new position, and take off garment. Take and stitch sleeve in, holding in a curve, with wrong side of garment and right side of sleeve head towards you. Machine with sleeve side on top. Don't clip turnings or trim closely; the slight constriction helps to keep the shape. Press sleeve head *only* from right side, as described.

*Raglan sleeve (figs 71a and b)*
This is ideal for children's clothes, being loose and easy to put on and take off. The side seams may be left open until the last, making manipulation and top stitching easy. Join shoulder dart or

overarm seam, and press turnings to one side, without trimming if to be top stitched. Keep top stitching within turning allowance. Set the sleeve to back and front armhole. Clip turnings alternately at underarm curve, and press open – or together for top stitching. Meeting notches, pin and stitch underarm and side seams together. Press well.

*Magyar sleeve (figs 72a–g)*
Used mainly for loose-fitting dresses, blouses and nightwear. But whether it's curved or cut at right angles, the underarm must be properly reinforced. For children's wear an inset gusset is strongest, and inserting a gusset isn't difficult. Mark end of slash, and place a 5 cm (2 in) square of non-woven interfacing centrally over it on wrong side, and tack. Machine a line from edge to tack, and down, as shown. Slash almost to point, and closely oversew point area. Stitch underarm and side seams. Pin gusset to pattern indications, tack and machine. For thin materials, trim and press turnings inwards. Cut a gusset in lining or self material, and press turnings under. Apply over gusset and hem to back of stitching. On thicker materials, press gusset turnings towards garment. From right side,

*Fig 72a Taping square underarm*

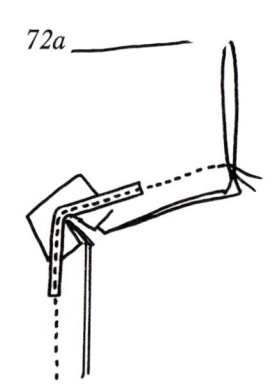

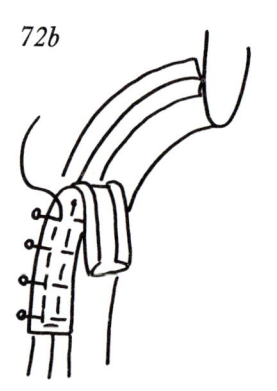

*Fig 72b Reinforcing curved underarm (inside)*

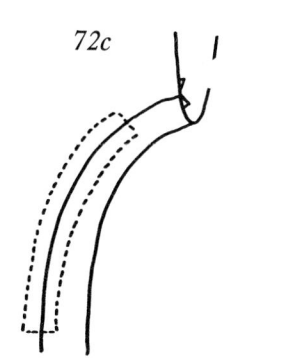

*Fig 72c Reinforcing curved underarm (outside)*

*Fig 72d Strengthening gusset position*

*Fig 72e Gusset position slashed*

*Fig 72f Fitting in gusset*

*Fig 72g Finished gusset edge stitched on outside*

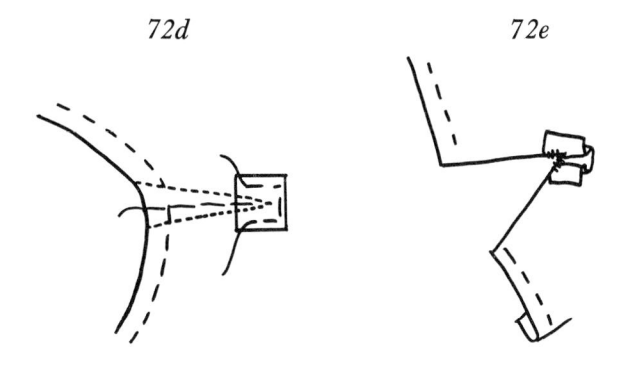

edge stitch round outside gusset seamline.

For square underarm, pin up seam and apply a square of non-woven interfacing over the angle. Machine seam, running narrow tape in over area of angle. Clip into corner and oversew. Press turnings apart (*fig 72a*). For curved underarm, stitch seam, clip turnings alternately, press apart. On inside, lay bias binding over opened turnings and tack both edges (*fig 72b*). On right side, machine close to seam to hold bind (*fig 72c*). This makes a strong, flat and comfortable underarm seam.

**Sleeve finishes**

There are many ways of finishing sleeve ends, but not all are suited to small children's clothes. Avoid tight sleeve ends, fiddly loops, tiny press-studs, hooks or buttons which are difficult to manage.

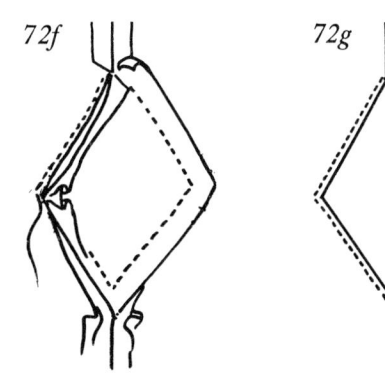

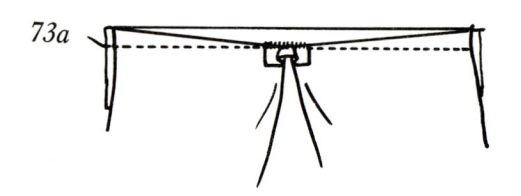

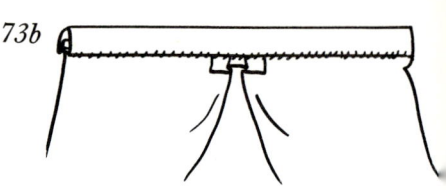

*Fig 73a Continuous lap opening stitched*

*Fig 73b Continuous lap opening neatened on inside*

Sleeves to be gathered into cuffs should be the child's full measurement from shoulder to wrist, plus 5 cm (2 in), and cuff depth added on to allow for full arm movement and growth. Suitable openings are:

*Continuous lap opening (figs 73a, b, and c)*
Both neat and strong. Mark top of opening, and tack a 5 cm (2 in) square of non-woven interfacing over it on inside. Slash to tack mark and closely oversew top of slash. Cut a strip of lengthwise material, 5 cm wide (2 in) by length of opening, plus 6 mm ($\frac{1}{4}$ in). Pin one edge along entire length of opening, right sides together, and tack. Starting 6 mm ($\frac{1}{4}$ in) from edge, machine towards point, as shown, with fullness folded towards yourself. At point, lower needle, and fold fullness away from you. Stitch to other end, widening out to 6 mm ($\frac{1}{4}$ in). Turn in free edge and slip hem fold to machine stitches. Close opening to form overwrap, with underlap extended. This placket is also suitable for girls' cotton skirts.

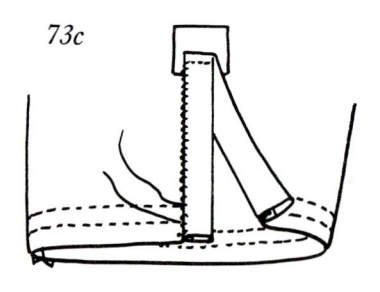

*Fig 73c Completed continuous lap opening (inside)*

*A faced slit opening*
Make this as described in chapter 12 but with 10 cm (4 in) opening.

**Cuffs** (*figs 74–78*)
Make with a 4 cm (approx 1$\frac{1}{2}$ in) extension. Gather bottom of sleeve with two rows, and draw up to fit cuff as far as extension. With right

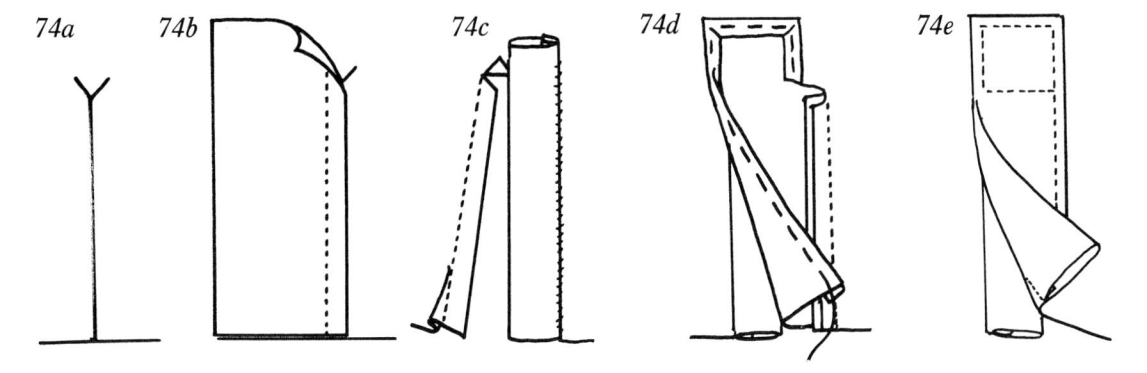

*Figs 74a, b, c, d, and e Stages in making a shirt cuff opening*

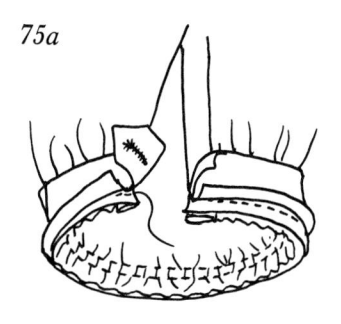

*Figs 75a and b Setting on a cuff*

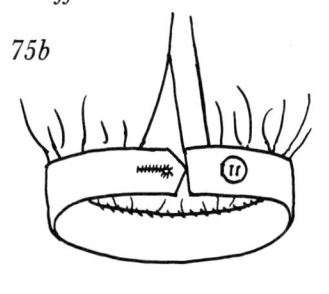

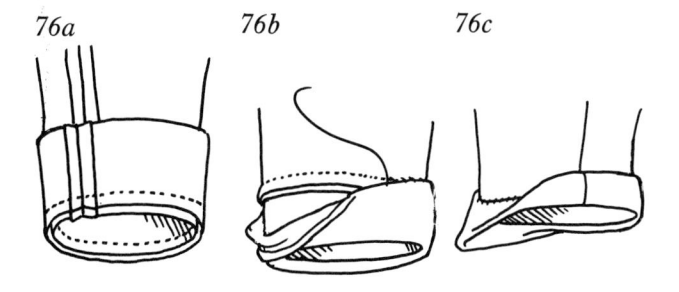

*Figs 76a, b, and c Simple cuff*

sides together, pin one edge of cuff to sleeve. Tack and stitch, then turn in free edge of cuff, and slip hem to machining inside. Make buttonhole(s) and sew on button(s). For linked buttons (on faced opening) allow extensions, and work buttonholes on both sides. Link the buttons with hat elastic. Cuffs may be made much deeper, to fold underneath to equalize wear, or to be turned down later to give added depth.

*Zipped sleeve opening*
Apply zip by central method at sleeve seam, as described in chapter 12. Neaten cuff edge, and enclose ends of zipper tape under sleeve hem.

*Cuff with no sleeve opening*
Remember that cuffs should be cut slightly larger than bottom edge of sleeves, if to be turned up. Make cuff in chosen style, and press well. For turned-up cuff in lightweight materials, pin right

side of cuff to wrong side of sleeve end. Stitch, and press turnings downwards. Turn in free edge of cuff, and slip hem to machine stitches on right side. Press, and turn cuff up, holding in place with strong tacks at sleeve seam.

*Cuff applied with a crossway facing (fig 77)*
Make cuff and place over sleeve end, right sides together. Cut 5 cm (2 in) wide crossway strip to fit cuff, join ends of facing, and neaten free edge. Place facing over cuff, wrong side uppermost, and machine all edges together. Trim and layer turnings. Turn facing to inside, rolling cuff down 1 cm ($\frac{3}{8}$ in) to conceal join. Catch free edge of facing.

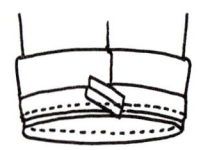

*Fig 77 Cuff applied with a crossway facing*

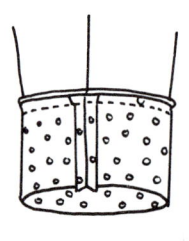

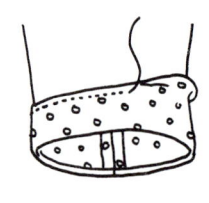

*Fig 78 Cuff faced on right side*

*Cuff faced on right side (fig 78)*
A decorative finish, and useful when material won't stretch to a proper hem. Cut and join facing strip in self or contrast material. Pin and tack right side of one facing edge to wrong side of sleeve edge on inside. Stitch, trim seam, and turn facing to right side. Turn under free edge, and tack down over sleeve. Press facing, and edge stitch tacked edge of facing.

*Elastic in slot for full sleeve ends*
A useful finish for thin materials. Turn up a small hem, and machine upper and lower edges, leaving 2·5 cm (1 in) open. Insert elastic, making sure that it won't constrict the child's arm.

# 12
# Openings and Fastenings

Choosing the right opening or fastening for children's clothes is particularly important. Such familiar mishaps as broken zips, and torn ends of plackets or pockets, are often due to them being too small to accommodate hasty, ever-growing little hands. Buttonholes, too, may be too small for the buttons used – or too fiddly for a child to manage. When planning these details, it's sensible to err on the generous side, and allow extra leeway.

**Measure first**
For front or back neck openings, measure round the child's head, and add at least 10 cm (4 in). Subtract the neck measurement of garment from this, and halve the remainder. The result is the proper length for opening. For skirt plackets, measure the child's hips round fullest part, and add 10 cm (4 in). Measure the waist, and subtract amount from 'hips – plus' measurement. Half this result gives correct placket length. Cuff openings should be sufficient to allow cuff to open flat.

**Zippers**
For children's wear, avoid nylon and 'invisible' zippers; only use lightweight ones for fine

materials, and use medium or heavyweight metal zips on jerkins and fly front openings – often the first casualties!

Split rings on slider ends will make zips easier for small children to manage. When putting in zips the commonest mistakes are (a) wavy, bulging zips (b) frilly, non-concealing edges of material (c) zips put in too tightly, causing 'bubbling' of edges either side. All these marks of the amateur can be avoided if correct precautions are taken for each method.

*Central method (figs 79a, b, and c)*
Turnings must be at least 1·5 cm ($\frac{5}{8}$ in) wide. Tack seam edges together, then, with largest stitch, machine from top to bottom of zipper opening. Change to normal stitch, and proceed to end of seam. Now, lay garment out, with wrong side uppermost, and place closed zip centrally in position over seam, with slider face down, its top 3 mm ($\frac{1}{8}$ in) below fitting line at waist or neck. Pin at top, and slightly ease material under zip-

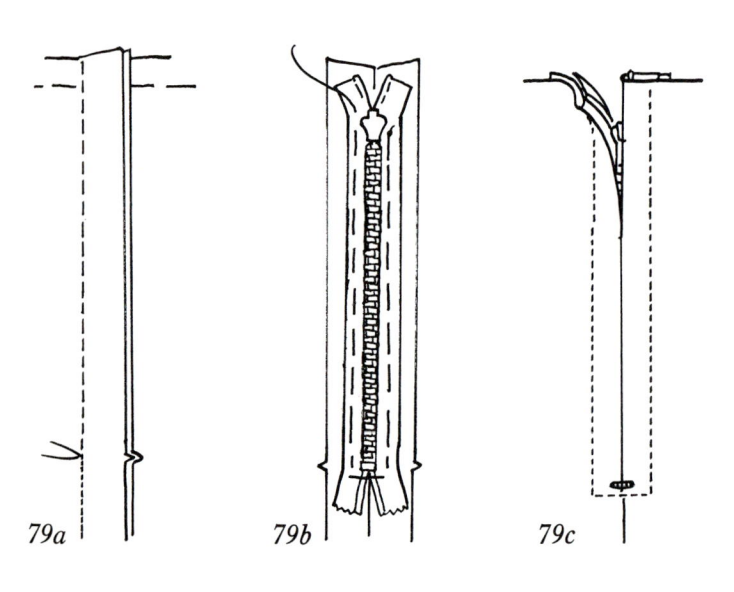

*Fig 79a Central method – zipper opening machined with long stitch*

*Fig 79b Zipper positioned inside*

*Fig 79c Right side of opening completed*

per. Press out fullness evenly; pin across bottom of zip, and at intervals between. Make sure that teeth lie centrally over the seam. Tack tape down both sides and across, below stop. From right side, machine round zip, keeping no less than 6 mm ($\frac{1}{4}$ in) from closed seam. Stitching too close makes for gaping edges. Remove tackings, and carefully unpick seam to within 6 mm ($\frac{1}{4}$ in) of zipper end. Result: a flat opening, with edges meeting exactly – an impossible feat if edges are merely overcast together!

Where waist seam crosses a zip, as on a full-length back opening, place turnings downwards, trimming closely. Use above method for centre front or back openings. Putting zips into centre back skirt seam is easier than at the side on a bias seam. Also, zip is put in before the garment is assembled.

*The lapped method (fig 80)*
Allow wide turnings of 2 cm ($\frac{3}{4}$ in) and apply seam binding inside fitting lines at zip position. Stitch seam up to placket opening. On back seam turn edge under 3 mm ($\frac{1}{8}$ in) outside fitting line. Place closed zip behind edge of fold, easing material slightly, and tack – teeth close to edge. Using a zipper foot, machine or hand back stitch on fold edge. Fold overwrap turning under, exactly on fitting line, press and tack. Place overwrap with fold edge just covering stitches on underside. Tack down. From inside, tack down edges of tape, and secure ends. Next, from outside stitch 1 cm ($\frac{3}{8}$ in) from edge of overwrap, across bottom below tack, and reverse. This calls for accuracy – or the needle may hit the teeth! Remove tacking, and blanket stitch bar tack at bottom (*fig 81*). Press well.

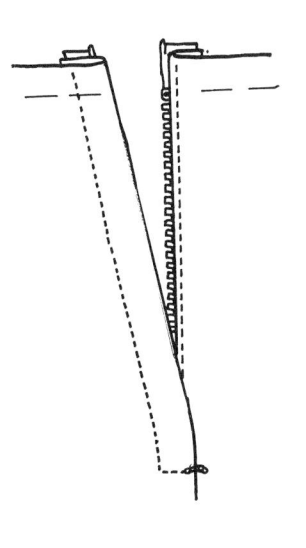

*Fig 80 Lapped method*

*Fig 81 Working a bar tack*

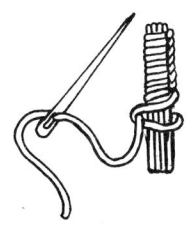

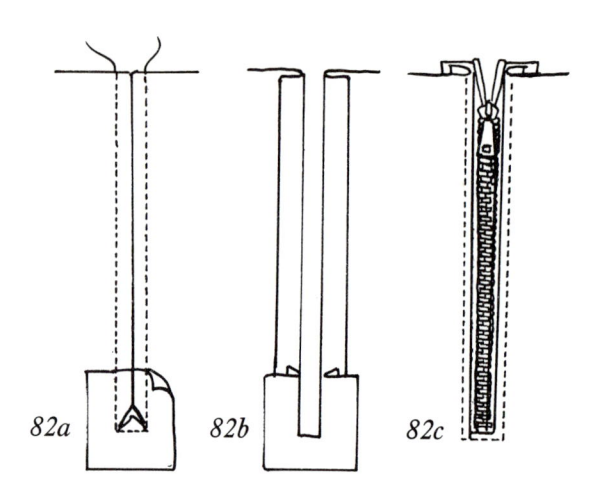

*Fig 82a Slot with facing applied on outside*

*Fig 82b Finished slot on inside*

*Fig 82c Zipper set into slot and edge stitched (outside)*

## Zipper in a slot (*figs 82a, b, and c*)
Mark or tack centre line of opening. On inside, apply a 5 cm (2 in) square of non-woven interfacing as shown. On outside, apply self material 6·5 cm (2½ in) centrally over bottom of opening, right sides together. Machine on tack line, and cut out slot, slashing into corners, and oversew these. Turn facing inside, shaping corners, and press. Pin and tack zipper behind slot, with slider 1·5 cm (⅝ in) below top edge. Edge stitch slot from right side as in *fig 82c*.

## Simulated leather
Stick interfacing in position on inside, and cut out slot shape accurately. Place zip behind slot, holding with sticky tape. Edge stitch on right side, as above.

## Faced opening (*figs 83a, b, and c*)
Used on neck and sleeve openings, with or without cuffs. Mark and prepare opening position with non-woven interfacing at bottom. Apply facing to right side. Rule two converging lines, starting at 6 mm (¼ in) from line at start of

*Fig 83a Facing applied to right side (outside)*

*Fig 83b Faced opening prepared (inside)*

*Fig 83c Finished opening on outside*

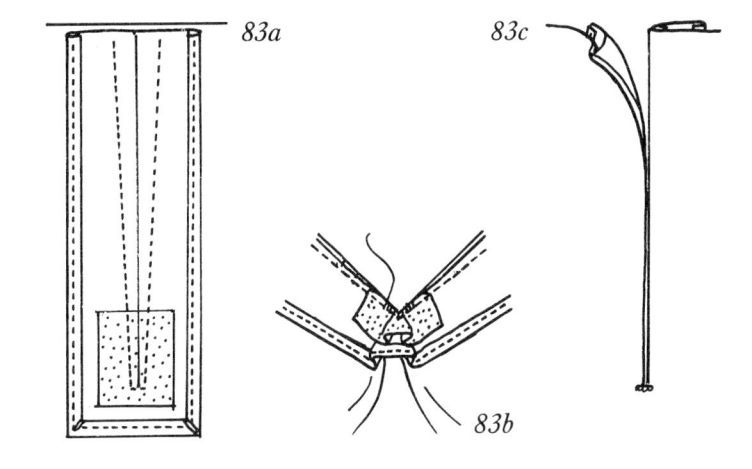

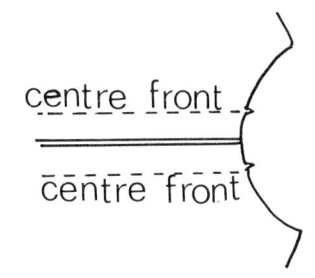

*Fig 84a Fly front opening*

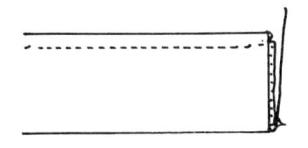

*Fig 84b Interfacing applied inside underwrap*

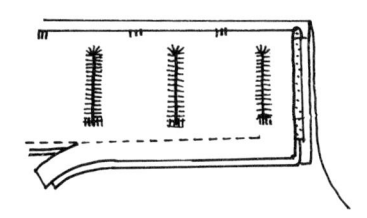

*Fig 84c Fly piece in position behind overwrap*

opening. Stitch to end of mark, taking two stitches across point, then up other side, widening to 6 mm ($\frac{1}{4}$ in). Slash centre, open slit and oversew point area. Turn facing inside, rolling seam line to inside, and neaten edge. Press.

*Fly front opening (figs 84a, b, c, and d)*
A neat and inconspicuous opening suitable for fronts of children's coats, jackets, jerkins etc. It's not difficult, but it does call for accuracy.

1 Make centre front line on both fronts. (Centre front opening is centre front of fly.) Average width of fly is 3·5 cm (approximately $1\frac{1}{4}$ in).

2 Cut fly piece twice required width, plus usual turnings. Fold lengthwise, right side outside, and press. Cut a 2·5 cm (1 in) strip of interfacing, and lay inside strip. Tack.

3 Mark buttonhole positions on fly with a maximum distance between them of 3·8 cm ($1\frac{1}{2}$ in). Hand or machine make buttonholes.

4 Place fly behind folded facing (right hand for a girl), with its fold edge 3 mm ($\frac{1}{8}$ in) from facing fold edge.

5 Tack and stitch through all thicknesses. Trim turnings and neaten.

6 Catch fold edge of fly to front facing just inside fold edge between buttonhole positions.

7 Apply interfacing behind facing allowance on left front and fold facing to inside.

8 Clip at neck for front opening, turn in and invisibly oversew top edges of facings.

9 Apply collar and/or facings at neck. (Note: For zipped fly on trousers, see chapter 15.) Velcro is an easy alternative for front fly opening on children's coats etc.

1 Prepare garment front facings as above, but don't fold under yet.

2 Apply smooth half of Velcro (to right side front facing allowance for girls) with outer edge just inside fold line. Hold with sticky tape and oversew both edges.

3 Apply hooked half outside of left front (not on facing allowance) with outer edge at facing fold line. Stitch both edges.

4 Fold facings to outside and stitch across top to clip at neck.

5 Turn facings to inside.

6 Tack and machine free edge of facing to fronts to hold, from right sides.

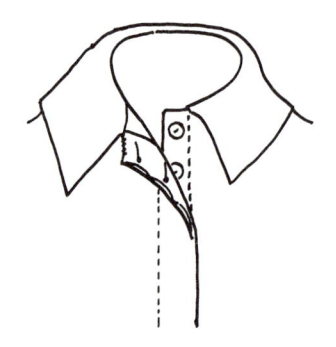

*Fig 84d Finished opening*

**Buttons and buttonholes**
Don't let those buttonholes be a bugbear! Good-looking buttonholes depend on absolutely accurate measurement at every stage. Careful preparation, and practice on spare material, whether

worked or bound buttonhole, is vital too. All buttonholes (and buttons) require an appropriate interfacing underneath. And always obtain buttons before making buttonholes – never guess at size! Remember, too, the thicker the button the bigger the buttonhole must be. The length of buttonhole equals its diameter, plus its thickness, plus 3 mm ($\frac{1}{8}$ in) for ease. Mark buttonhole positions so that edge of button, when attached, comes no nearer than 1·3 cm ($\frac{1}{2}$ in) to fold edge. Use matching thread, rubbed through beeswax.

*Fig 85 Stages in working a buttonhole*

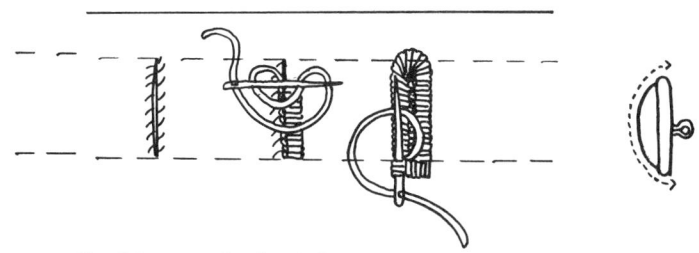

*Worked buttonholes (fig 85)*
After spacing and marking, cut slit and lightly overcast edges. Starting at end farthest from garment edge, insert needle below slash from inside, bringing out 3 mm ($\frac{1}{8}$ in) above slash, keeping thread under needle at eye and at point. Pull upwards, forming knot at cut edge. At round end, fan stitches out, keeping same distance from slit. At straight end, take several blanket stitches right across. Vertical buttonholes have two straight ends.

Automatic attachments cope well with buttonholes nowadays, but here, too, practice is essential before embarking on garments.

*Plain bound buttonholes (fig 86)*
Prepare positions as above. Cut a strip of fabric exactly along a thread 5 cm (2 in) wide by 5 cm

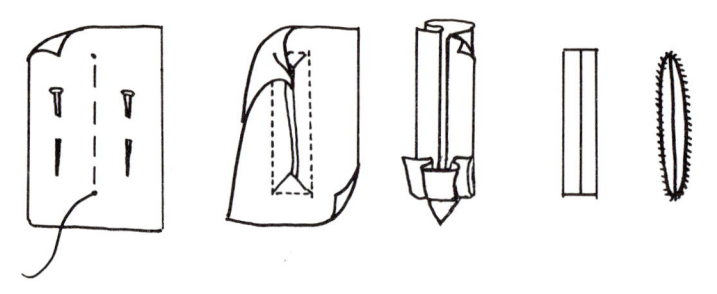

*Fig 86 Stages in making a bound buttonhole*

(2 in) longer than buttonhole. Fold strip lengthwise along a thread, right side outside, and lay fold to centre mark of buttonhole. Open and tack down. Starting nearest to edge, machine a rectangle, going over first end again, and counting stitches to be sure of a perfect rectangle. Cut slit to within 6 mm ($\frac{1}{4}$ in) of ends and clip diagonally into corners. Pull strip to inside, shaping corners. Form two equal pleats, and turn in tiny triangles at ends. Tack through from right side. Machine or backstitch along seam line. Press well (turnings away from slot). Fold and tack facing in place over buttonholes. From right side, push a pin through each end of buttonhole. On inside, cut facing between pins, turn edges under, and oversew, rolling material under at ends. Press well.

*Fabric loops (figs 87a and b, 88a and b)*
For small children, avoid tiny loops set close together. Cut a sufficiently long strip of crossway material, approximately 3·2 cm ($1\frac{1}{4}$ in) wide. Fold lengthwise, right side inside, pin, and stitch. Trim turnings. Using strong thread in a bodkin join on at one end. Pass bodkin into tube and pull through to right side. For extra strength, thread cord back into tube and leave. Cut loops, measured over button, plus 2·5 cm (1 in) for joining on. Space out and mark positions on a piece of paper, apply loops, and hold in position

*Fig 87a Making piping for fabric loops*

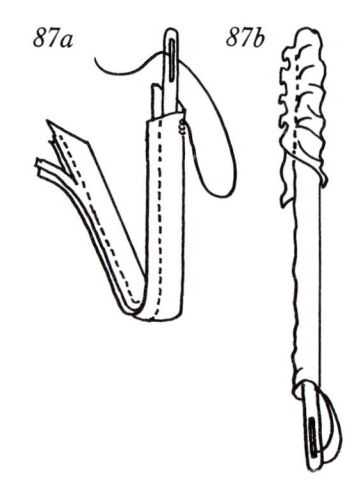

87a       87b

*Fig 87b Turning piping right side out with a bodkin*

*Fig 88a Loops held down with sticky tape*

*Fig 88b Loops stitched to garment and faced*

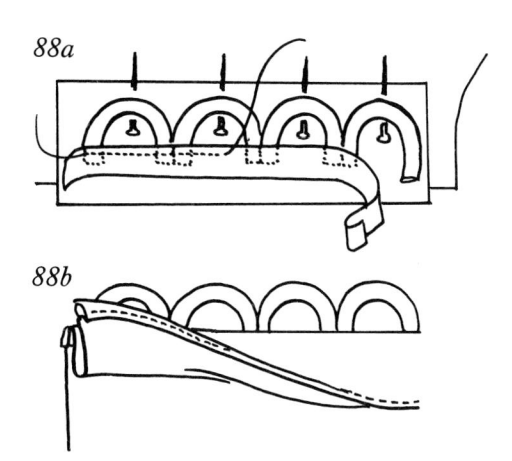

*88a*

*88b*

with sticky tape behind seam line mark. Pin paper to right side of garment edge, and stitch. Peel off sticky tape and tear away paper. Apply facing, and stitch. Fold facing inside, and press. Fabric loops are stronger than worked chains for belt carriers. Set them into side seams, stitching twice.

*Hooks and eyes*
These are not ideal for children's clothing. If used, avoid tiny ones, and don't use on loose weaves, or holes will soon appear. Work blanket (loop) stitch closely over entire eyelets of hook and eye. Oversew hook right up to the bend. Where edges are to meet, place loop with bend slightly back from edge, and loop projecting a little.

*Press studs*
Here, too, use blanket stitch – at least six – through each hole. Make sure that ball and socket exactly coincide when opening is closed. Use hole in ball to align with socket by putting a pin through to underlap.

*Toggles and frogging*
See chapter 16.

# 13
# Pockets are Important

Children always make full use of their pockets, so do make them sufficiently wide and deep, with reinforced corners and interfacing underneath.

For children's garments the most practical types are:

1 Patch pockets, with or without flaps.

2 Inset pockets with zipped opening.

3 Bound one-piece pockets.

4 Pockets incorporated in side seams.

**Preparation**
For all types, apply a non-woven interfacing strip 5 cm (2 in) wide, by 5 cm (2 in) longer than pocket opening, behind pocket position. Where suitable, extend interfacing into seams for extra strength. Always use long tailor tacks to mark pairs of pockets to ensure identical positioning on both sides. Make sure that pockets are not placed too high or too low, and are easily accessible without pulling at garment – a point often overlooked.

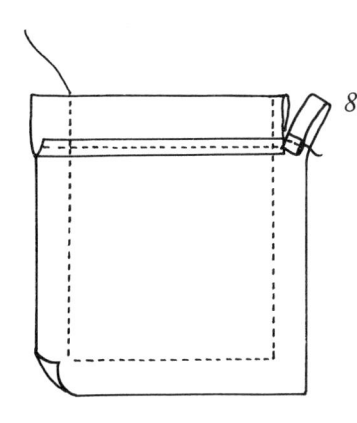

*Figs 89a, b, and c Making a lightweight patch pocket*

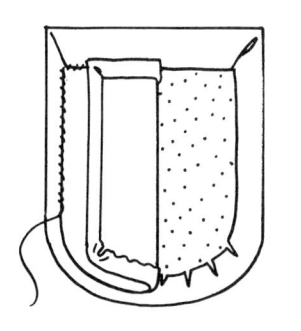

*Fig 90 Patch pocket interfaced and lined*

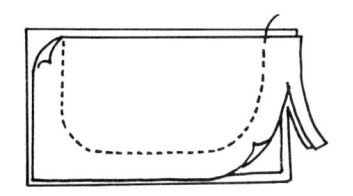

*Fig 91 Making a flap*

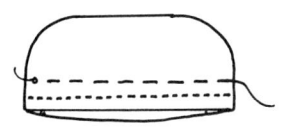

*Fig 92 Finished flap*

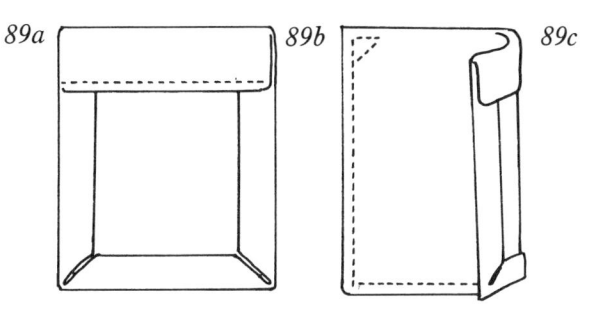

## Types of pocket

*Patch pocket (figs 89a, b, c, and 90)*
Prepare position and cut pockets to desired shape, allowing normal turnings, except on top edge where you should add 2·5 cm (1 in). Turn down top edge 6 mm ($\frac{1}{4}$ in) and stitch. Fold over on to right side at top fold line and stitch sides of turndown. On curved pockets, notch seam allowance and press turnings inside. On square pockets, trim off 6 mm ($\frac{1}{4}$ in) at lower corners, mitre them and turn in seam allowance. Press. Apply pocket to garment, and edge stitch, forming triangles at top corners as shown. On thicker materials, cut interfacings, minus turnings, to pocket shape, and tack to inside of pocket. Fold in turnings, and turn down top on fold line, sloping inwards. Catch turnings lightly to interfacing (*fig 90*), and press. On coats, line pocket too. Apply pocket, and top stitch 1 cm ($\frac{3}{8}$ in) from edge. For an added flap, (*figs 91 and 92*), cut material double (on thinner materials) with layer of light interfacing and stitch on three sides, trim interfacing almost to stitching, and treat turnings as described. Turn flap to right side, rolling seam slightly to inside. Press, and trim top edges level. Apply flap, right sides together, 1·5 cm ($\frac{5}{8}$ in) above top of pocket, stitching 1·3 cm ($\frac{1}{2}$ in) from edge. Turn flap down and press. Top stitch

6 mm (¼ in) from join, or hold flap down with a bar tack at each corner. On thicker materials, cut material single, interface, and line pocket flap.

*Inset pocket with or without a zipper*
Used mainly on anoraks, jerkins, and jackets of leather or vinyl-backed materials. *Figs 93, and 94a and b* show how to make the pocket without a zipper. The following instructions include a zipper.

*On woven cloth.* Mark pocket position and interface the area inside. Cut a facing the length of pocket plus 5 cm (2 in) and apply centrally over mark, right sides together. Mark out an accurate rectangle the length of pocket by 1·5 cm (⅝ in) and stitch. Slash down centre to within 6 mm (¼ in) of ends and snip diagonally into corners (*fig 95a*). Turn facing inside, rolling seam slightly. Tack and press. Apply zipper behind slot, as described in chapter 12. Stitch closely round edge on right side *fig. 95b*. Cut two pocket pieces 5 cm (2 in) longer than opening, one 14 cm (5½ in) and one 18 cm (7 in) deep. Turn in top edge of shorter piece, and apply fold to machining below zip inside. Fold in top edge of longer piece, place to stitching above zipper, and oversew (*fig 96*). Turn raw edge up again, shape pocket bag, tack and stitch edges together. Overcast or zig-zag to neaten (*fig 97*).

*Zipped pocket in vinyl or leather.* Inset zipper as described in chapter 12. Cut pocket bag as for cloth, above.

*Bound pocket*
Interface behind pocket area. Cut binding piece and pocket in one 5 cm (2 in) wider than pocket opening by 28 cm (11 in). Place over pocket

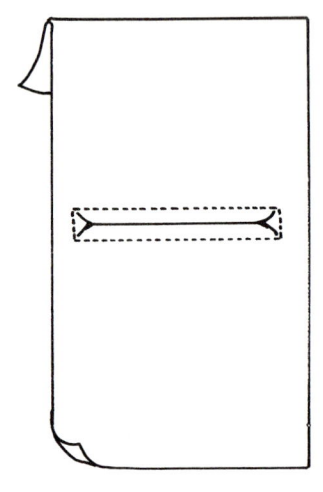

*Fig 93 One piece pocket bag sewn to outside – opening stitched and cut*

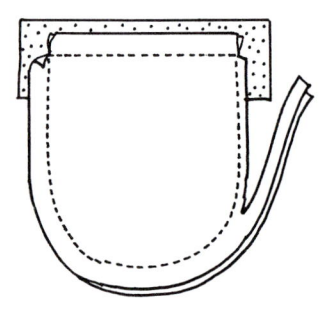

*Fig 94a Finished pocket bag (inside)*

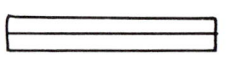

*Fig 94b Finished pocket (outside)*

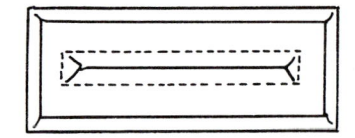

*Fig 95a Inset pocket with zipper. Facing applied on outside*

*Fig 95b Zipper set into slot and edge stitched on outside*

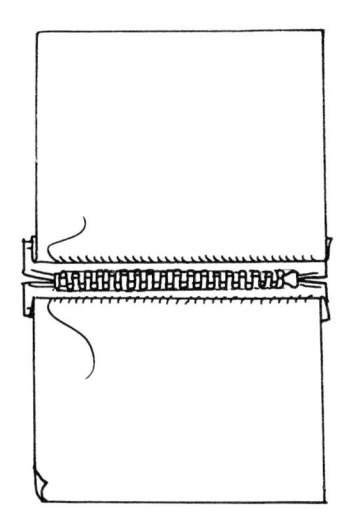

*Fig 96 Pocket bag pieces hemmed to zipper tape on inside and oversewn on outside*

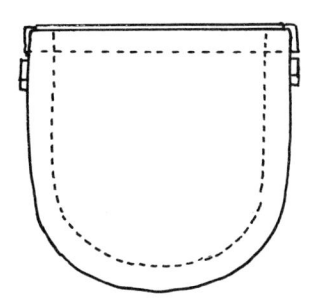

*Fig 97 bag shaped and neatened*

*Fig 98 Pocket in side seam. Interfacing applied inside seam line*

*Figs 99a and b Applying pocket bag*

mark, right sides together, with top half 2·5 cm (1 in) longer than lower half. Stitch a rectangle, cut and pull through as for cloth slot. Press turnings away from slot and form even binds with inverted pleats at ends. Stitch from right side just outside seam. On inside, fold down upper half of bag, trim edges, stitch and neaten. Work bar tacks at either end on right side (*see fig 81*).

*Pocket incorporated in side seam*
Cut four strips of non-woven interfacing 5 cm (2 in) longer than pocket opening by 2·5 cm (1 in) wide, and baste to seam line inside back and fronts of garments at pocket positions (*fig 98*). Cut pocket pieces to shape. On back halves of pocket apply a 7·5 cm (3 in) piece of self material, right side of material to right side of pocket, turn in lower edge and edge stitch. Place faced halves to right side of garment back and stitch on seam line. Apply front halves, right sides together, to fronts of garments, and stitch 6 mm ($\frac{1}{4}$ in) outside seam line. Stitch up side seams above and below pockets (*figs 99a and b*). Turn pocket pieces inside, folding front edge exactly on seam line.

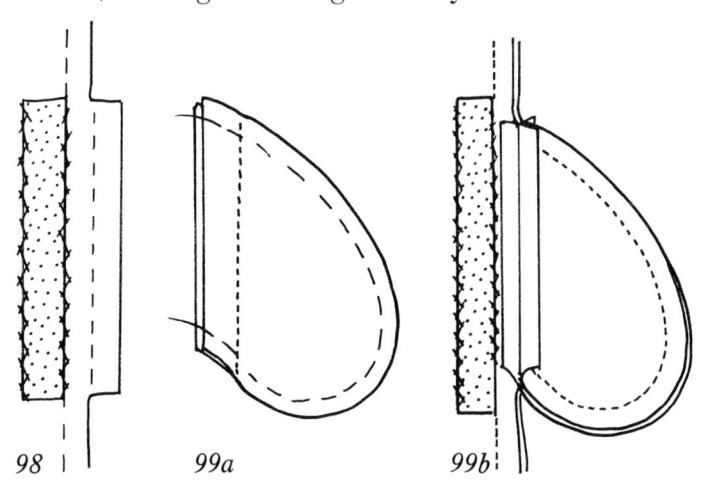

Stitch pocket halves together and fold towards front. Press well, and work bar tacks on outside at ends of opening.

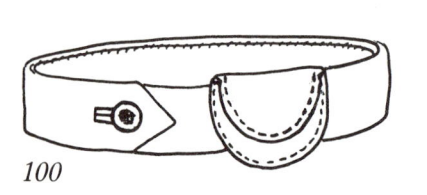

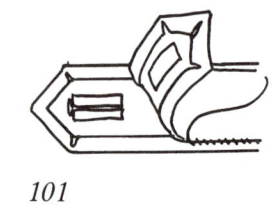

*Fig 100 Pocket on a belt*

*Fig 101 Belt detail*

*Pocket in a belt*
Where a little girl's dress has no pockets, why not make a belt in self or contrasting material with its own built-in pocket (*fig 100*)? Children love these. Cut the belt fairly wide, and interface with stiff non-woven interfacing (*fig 101*). Cut two oval shapes and two lower halves interfacing, as in *figs 102a and b*. Tack layers together. Turn raw edges of oval shape inwards and tack. Edge stitch the upper half only. Trim off corners and turn in edges of lower half. Oversew straight edges. Place on the oval, tack and edge stitch both portions of pocket together. Fasten off threads and press well. Close with small square of Velcro (*fig 103*), or a press stud. Attach to belt with double line of stitching at top of flap.

*Figs 102a and b Making a pocket*

*Fig 103 Finished pocket with Velcro squares for fastening*

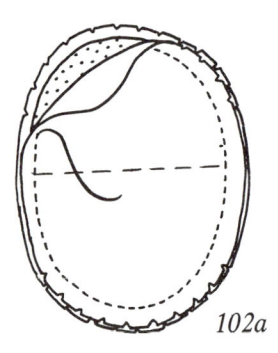

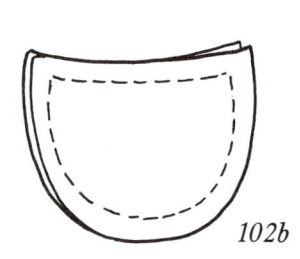

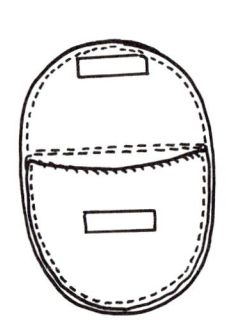

# 14

# Hems can Let You Down

Hems that look home-made are a real let-down. Yet we so often see hems that waver up and down at front, back or sides, with stretched edges, ridges on the right side and bulges on the wrong side; hems that are too narrow or too wide for the material, or for the width of the hemline. But all these marks of the amateur are so easy to avoid, if the right techniques are used.

Uneven hems are often due to faulty measuring, or the material dropping where it falls on the bias. We all know the difficulties of trying to pin up a hem on a fidgety child, but if the pattern has already been checked, and the finished length decided upon, it's merely a matter of trying on the finished garment, and checking the distance from floor to the proposed turn-up line – not of levelling the hem, or of turning it up on the child. That is sure to be difficult! With a long ruler or a patent hem marker, pin or mark the distance from the ground where the fold is to be. That's all.

Take off the garment, and lay it out on a table. With a notched strip of card, mark with chalk or pins the desired amount of hem depth, measured from your chalk-marked or pinned fold line. Any slight variation in the amount to be turned up will be cut off as you trim edges level with your markings. Be sure, while measuring, that the child is standing quite naturally – not stiffened up. If the garment has a belt or ties, fasten them.

**Points to consider**
As a rule, the narrower the hemline, the deeper the hem, but with children's clothes a fairly deep hem is usually wanted, eg 5 cm (2 in) minimum. On very thin materials, make a double or even a treble hem. Don't allow a 'half allowance' to show through.

On long party dresses, a fairly deep hem will make the garment hang better. But on frills and ruffles in filmy material, make the tiniest possible hem, either hand-rolled, or machined on the edge. Bias cut dresses and skirts should always be hung up overnight before finally testing the hem length, to allow the seams and bias weave to drop.

Techniques vary according to the material, and whether the hem is straight or curved. Whatever method is used, seam turnings should be pressed flat, and opened to where hem turn-up will lie. Put in all pins at right angles to edge.

**Types of hem**

*Straight hem (fig 104)*
For cottons and other light materials. Fold hem allowance up, and tack near fold edge. Lay garment on padded board, and place a strip of cardboard under raw edge. Turn edge under 1·5 cm ($\frac{5}{8}$ in) and press in a crease. Pin or tack down 1 cm ($\frac{3}{8}$ in) from edge. Working from left to right, take up a single thread from the garment, pass needle

*Fig 104 Straight hem*

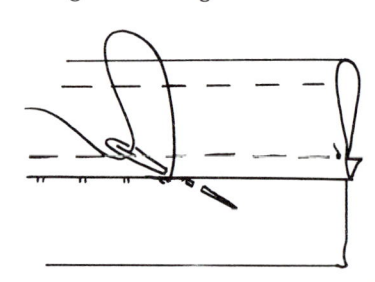

through fold, and bring it out. Take next stitch through garment, and so on. Don't pull thread tightly.

*Quick hand-rolled hem for frills in sheer materials (fig 105)*
Fold edge 1 cm (⅜ in) down. Now take a tiny stitch on the folded edge, then one on the single fabric below, but slightly in front of the previous one, as shown. At every 2·5 cm (1 in) hold the fold down firmly, and gently pull up the thread. You'll get a nicely rolled ege.

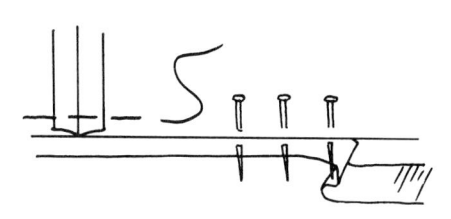

*Fig 105 Quick hand-rolled hem*

*Fig 106 Seam bound hem*

*Seam bound hem (fig 106)*
Seam binding is only suitable for straight, or nearly straight hems. Pin seam binding in place on right side, but tack from wrong side of hem edge. This will ensure that binding is not stitched too near the hem edge, and won't break out in wear.

*Faced hems*
Useful when material is short, and for lengthening. For facing the wrong side, use lining or similar matching material. Facing the right side with contrasting bands can add interest, especially if used on cuffs as well (see chapter 11). Cut facing band, shaped to curve of hem, and width required, plus turnings. Joins must coincide with side seams. Turn one edge down 1·5 cm (⅝ in), and crease fold.

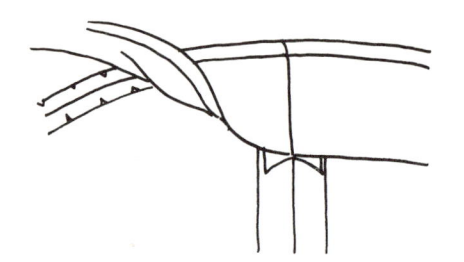

*Fig 107 Hem faced on inside (false hem)*

*Facing on inside (false hem) (fig 107)*
Place facing, right sides together, raw edges level, to hemline. Tack and stitch 1·5 cm (⅝ in) from edge. Press turnings open, and roll seam line slightly to inside. Press crease, and tack and catch stitch upper edge of facing to garment inside.

*Facing on outside (decorative)*
Apply band, prepared as above, to wrong side of garment with its right side to inside. Stitch, and press turnings open. Fold band on to outside of garment, tack folded edge in place and edge stitch.

*Tailor's hem (fig 108)*
Used on thick materials to prevent a ridge showing on right side. Overcast, pink, or bind raw hem edge. On wrong side, turn up hem, and tack near upper edge, and again near hem edge. Working from left to right, roll back edge 6 mm (¼ in) and take a tiny stitch in garment, then one from inside hem edge alternately, keeping edge rolled down as you work. Keep thread slack. Press hem at fold edge only, and remove tackings. No stitches should show.

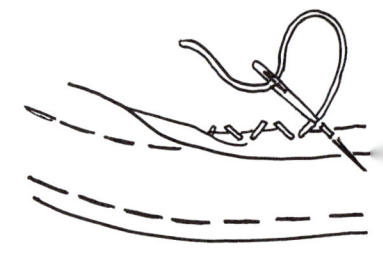

*Fig 108 Tailor's hem*

*Fig 109 Loop stitching a hem on jersey material*

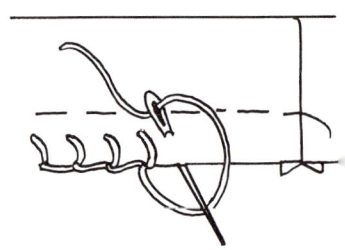

*Hem on jersey materials (fig 109)*
Turn up hem and tack into position 1·3 cm (½ in) from raw edge. With pure silk or synthetic

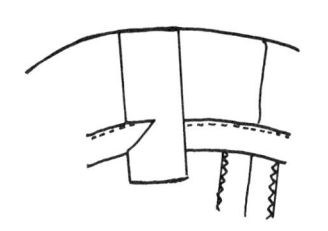

*Fig 110 Curved hem using cardboard marker*

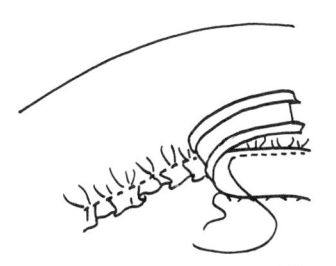

*Fig 111 Curved hem with crossway binding*

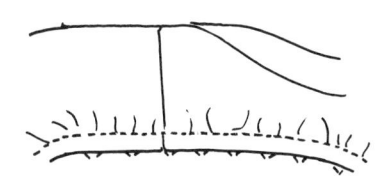

*Fig 112 Curved hem on cottons*

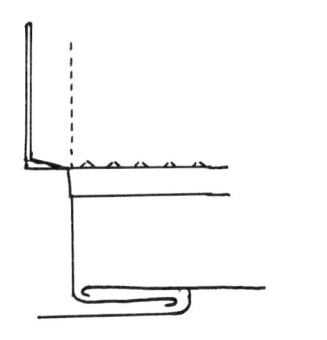

*Fig 113 Hem that includes a pleat*

thread, work three blanket (loop) stitches on raw edge only. Take every fourth stitch through garment – single thread – only. This is slow, but produces satisfactory and elastic hem finish which won't break out in wear.

*Curved hems (figs 110 and 111)*
These can cause problems unless properly dealt with. The turned-up part is necessarily fuller than the part it is sewn to – the more curved and deeper the hem, the greater the amount of surplus fullness to be eased, gathered, or shrunk to fit. On wool cloth, run a gathering thread along edge and draw up to fit. Place a shaped piece of cardboard, wider than hem, under gathered edge, and shrink away fullness (*fig 110*). (See chapter 7.) Neaten edge with crossway binding (*fig 111*), turn up, and loosely catch stitch hem to garment. Unshrinkable materials must be eased evenly on binding.

*Curved hem on cottons (fig 112)*
Turn down a tiny single hem and press it. With a loose tension and large stitch, machine on edge. Turn up hem, pin and tack in place. Draw gathers up to fit by under thread, arranging fullness evenly. Slip hem to garment and press.

*Hem that includes a pleat (fig 113)*
This can look clumsy – but here's the trick. Clip the pleat seam exactly where top of turn-up will come, trim and press open turnings below clip. Turn up hem and slip stitch to garment. Oversew bottom of turnings at clip. Position pleat from inside, keeping turnings together. Press pleat from both sides, and the hem on fold edge only.

*Blouse hem (figs 114a, b, and c)*
Turn under and edge stitch hem and front facings. Fold facings on to the fronts. Stitch and trim off. Turn facings to inside, fold up and tack hem in place. Slip hem to garment.

*Top stitched hem*
A decorative hem finish for thick, velour type or bonded coating materials. Turn hem approximately 2·5–3 cm (1–1½ in). Tack and press well. Machine two or more rows of top stitching on right side.

*Interfaced hem (fig 115)*
Used to stiffen and hold hem out, eg on flared coats, skirts of party dresses etc. Cut non-woven interfacing 2·5 cm (1 in) wider than actual hem, and place to fold line of hem. Catch down interfacing lightly at both edges. Garment hem is herringboned to interfacing only, so garment hem depth is invisible from right side. (See also chapter 17.)

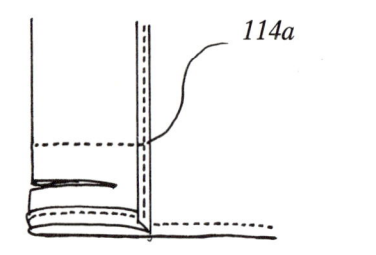

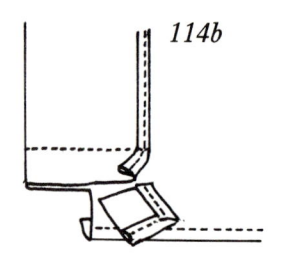

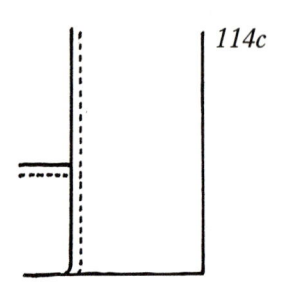

*Figs 114a, b, and c How to make a blouse hem*

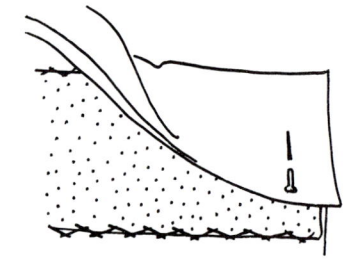

*Fig 115 Interfaced hem*

# 15
# Coveralls, Jeans and Trousers

Clothes for play, generally messing about, and informal sports must be functional and tough, but they needn't be dull or conventional. With toddlers, the main hazard to clothing is spilling. Although vinyl-coated materials are ideal for outdoor water play, they're not so good for food spills, which merely roll off on to carpets! Bright towelling is more suitable. One hand towel will make an attractive cover-up.

**Towel turnabout** (*figs 116a and b*)
Fold towel in half widthwise, and cut a hole in centre of fold to accommodate child's head comfortably. Bind edges with crossway binding. Try

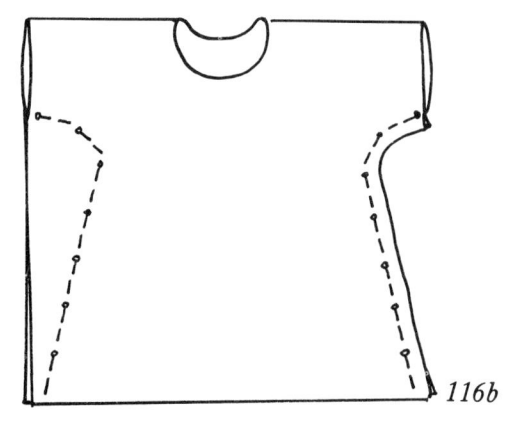

*Figs 116a and b Towelling turnabout*

on, with wrong side outside, and put in pins around one underarm and down side, well away from body. Remove, and pin other side. Cut to shape, allowing generous turnings. Tack and stitch. Clip turnings at underarm curve, and reinforce area with binding (see chapter 9). Use cuttings to make patch pockets. Neaten side seams. Make hem if required, or leave bottom as towel finish.

**Plastic raincoat into coverall** (*fig 117*)
Don't discard the toddler's raincoat when collar or armholes get torn. Instead, carefully remove collar and sleeves (*fig 118*), and bind cut edges. Unpick, and remove patch pockets. Worn back to front, the useless raincoat makes an ideal coverall when playing with paints, clay, water etc.

**Easy dirndl skirt or apron** (*figs 119a, b, and c*)
You'll need one width of 122 cm (48 in) printed cotton for ages six to eight years, or 90 cm (36 in) wide for three to five years. To find amount required, measure child from waist to desired hemline, adding 10 cm (4 in) for hem and top turning. Buy draw-up curtain tape to fit width of material.

*Making up*
Join selvedges together, and put in an 18 cm (7 in) zip by central method (see chapter 12). Fold under 1·5 cm ($\frac{5}{8}$ in) at top edge and press crease. Pin and stitch on tape, turning in at ends. Make a 7·5 cm (3 in) hem at bottom. Draw up cords to fit child's waist, and knot them well away from opening. Sew on hook and eye at top of zip. (Apron – hem selvedges, sew on tape as above. Turn up bottom hem, and fasten at back waist with two buttons and worked loops.)

*Fig 117 Coverall made from a plastic raincoat*

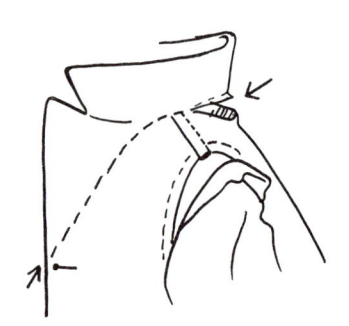

*Fig 118 How to remove the collar from a raincoat*

*Figs 119a, b, and c*
*Making a girl's dirndl skirt from a remnant*

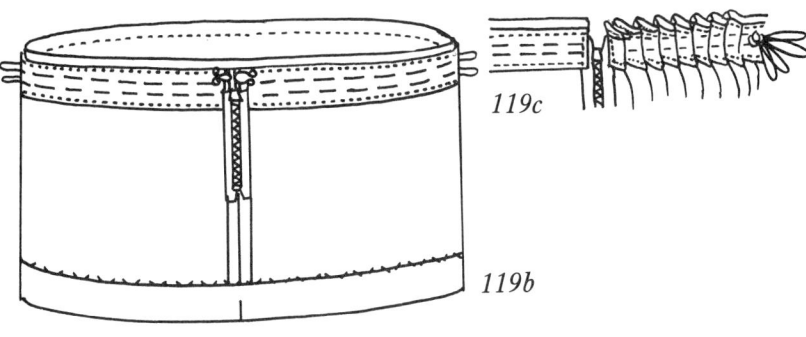

**Toddler's dungarees** (*figs 120a, b, c, and d*)
To allow ample room for bulky nappies, without making legs unduly sloppy, let in extra seat space by a simple alteration to a trouser pattern, as shown. Add up to 10 cm (4 in) as required (chapter 2). Cut out and make up trousers, leaving underleg seam open, and sew on tape with snap fasteners for easier changing. Cut bib double, and stitch on three sides. Trim seam, and turn outside. Lay raw edges of bib to front waist, edges level, and stitch. Try on, and decide length for straps. Make and press these. At back waist,

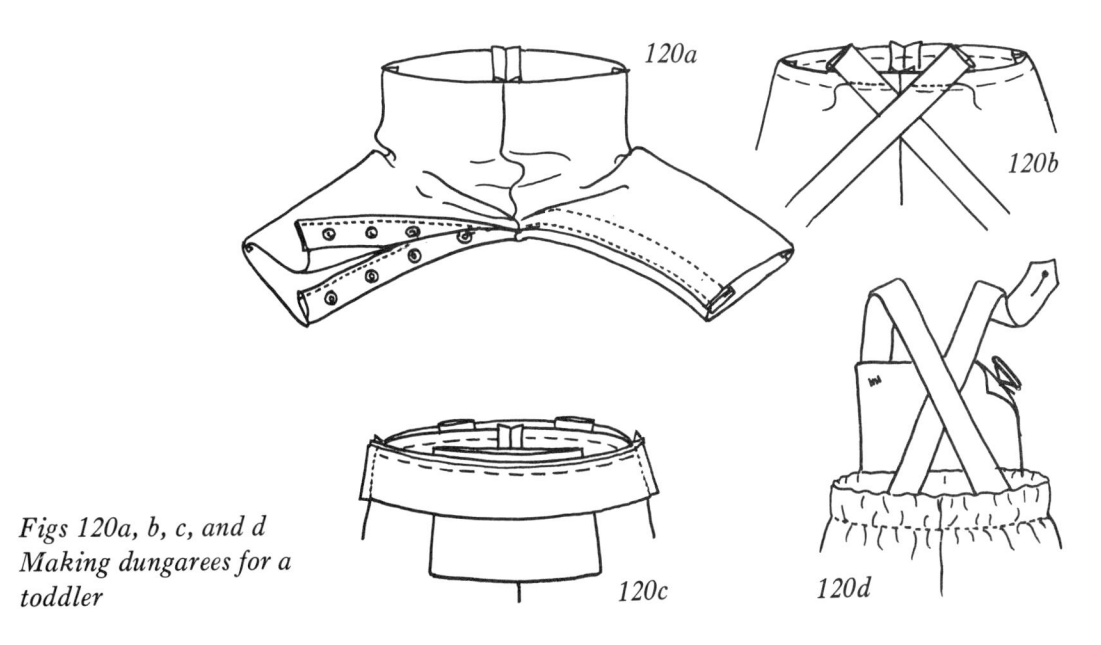

*Figs 120a, b, c, and d*
*Making dungarees for a toddler*

arrange open ends in slanting position, 10 cm (4 in) apart, cross straps, trim edges level with waist edge, stitch (*120b*). Cut waist facing 5 cm (2 in) wide to fit waist, and join. With straps and bib placed downwards, pin facing to waist edge on outside, stitch (*120c*). Turn facing inside, fold free edge under, and tack and machine on fold edge, leaving 2·5 cm (1 in) open for inserting wide elastic to fit child's waist comfortably. Sew buttons at each corner of bib, and work buttonholes at ends of straps (chapter 12).

**Older child's jeans and trousers** (*fig 121*)
Easier to make professionally than you may think! First essential is a good basic pattern, tested and adjusted to fit the child, and preferably transferred on to non-woven interfacing (chapter 2). For jeans, buy best-quality denim – cheap buys are no bargain here. Youngsters may like their jeans skin-tight – *you* want them to last a reasonable time. So steal a march and soak material overnight in cold water first! Cut out, marking indications. Stitch and press all darts.

*Front opening* (*figs 122a, b, c, and 123*)
This is easier if done before garment is assembled. Pin fronts together, tack and stitch from crotch to start of opening. Buy a special sturdy jean zip if you can find one. Make sure it is the correct length. The top of slider must come slightly below waist seam line. Fold extensions under on seam line of both fronts, and tack. Press. With right sides together, stitch curved edge of flypieces. Trim, notch, and turn to outside. Press. Place closed zip, face up, behind right side (as worn) just concealing stitching, and tack through fold. From inside, on extension only,

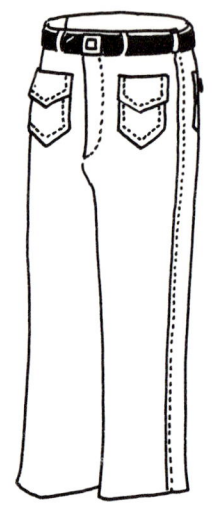

*Fig 121 Jeans for an older child*

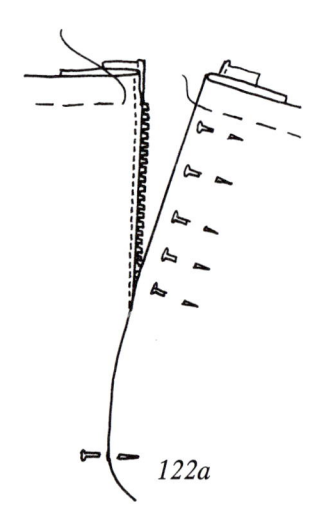

*Fig 122a Zipper stitched to underside of front opening*

*Fig 122b Zipper stitched to overwrap (inside)*

*Fig 122c Front opening stitched through all thicknesses*

*Fig 123 Finished front opening (outside)*

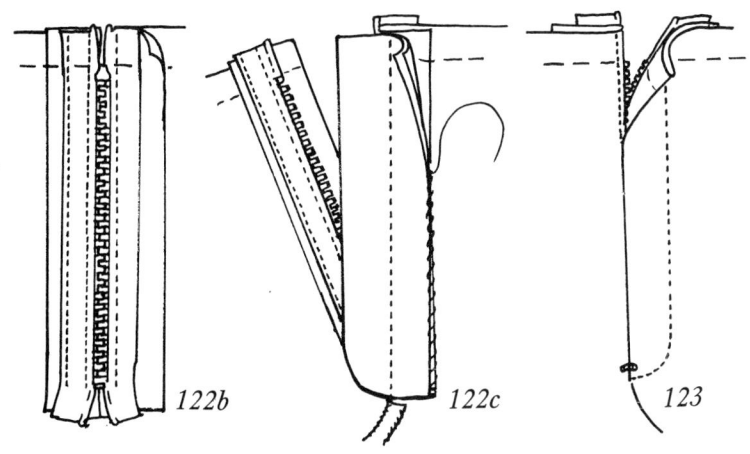

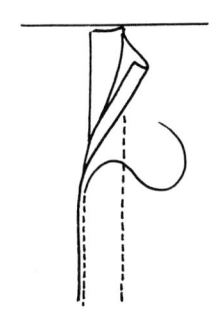

*Fig 124 Run and fell seam, top stitched outside*

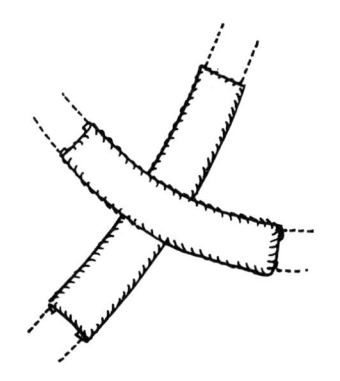

*Fig 125 Crotch neatened with crossway binding*

stitch zip close to teeth, and again 6 mm (¼ in) away. Fold extension down, and tack, curving to seam. Now, from outside, stitch beside tacked line through all thicknesses. Open zip, and place fly piece to underside extension, raw edges level, and stitch. Trim and neaten edges. Work a bar at bottom of opening on outside.

*Making up*
Join side seams on outside. Press turnings to one side, trim down under layer, and press untrimmed layer over it, turning in raw edge 6 mm (¼ in). Tack down. With white button thread or buttonhole twist, on top only, and using large stitch, machine on fold edge (*fig 124*). Make and apply pockets (chapter 13), top stitching to match seams. Stitch leg seams, and remainder of back to front seam, in same manner. Stretch – don't clip – curved portions. Reinforce crotch with crossway binding (*fig 125*). Cut waistband to fit jeans waist (including fly facing), and 10 cm (4 in) wide. Fold lengthwise, stitch across ends, and turn to outside. Press. Cut and stitch six belt carriers 2·5 cm (1 in) by 6·6 cm (2½ in). Arrange with one end to waist edge, and secure. Place

119

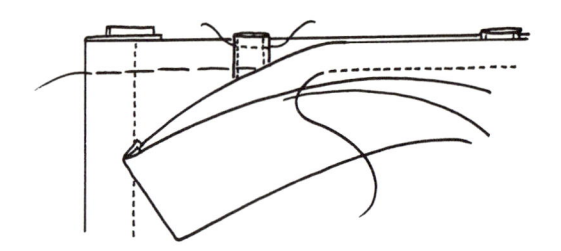

*Fig 126 Attaching the waistband*

waistband to garment, right sides together, edges level, and stitch (*fig 126*). Turn free edge inside, fold under 1·3 cm (½ in) and hem to stitching. On outside, fold under top edge of carriers at fold of waistband, and tack. Edge stitch entire waistband. Apply metal trouser hook and bar inside waistband (*fig 127*). Test jeans for correct length. Turn up, and press hems.

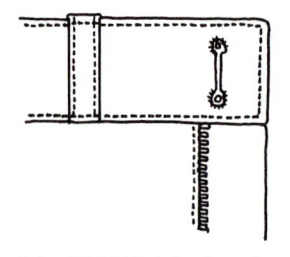

*Fig 127 Finished waistband with carrier*

**Corduroy trousers**
Corduroy looks richer if cut with pile running up. Cut out, and mark trousers. Make front opening as jeans, lining flypiece with thinner material. Make open seams, and omit belt carriers, if preferred. Make pockets in side seams (chapter 13). Otherwise, complete as for jeans. Press lightly on wrong side (chapter 7).

# 16
# Anoraks and Duffle Coats

These indispensable unisex items are acceptable wear for almost any occasion nowadays. Though quite expensive to buy, both garments are easy to make. Fitting problems are few; looseness and comfort are of first importance.

**Anoraks**
Ready quilted material padded with Terylene or Fortrel wadding is available in most colours, in wide, economical widths. Adapting a plain coat or jacket pattern is simple. First, pin the unaltered pattern together at seamlines of sides and shoulders, also sleeve seams, and try on the child over a chunky pullover or cardigan. Place centre front line accurately. If the fit is snug, enlarge the pattern, allowing 15 cm (6 in) to child's chest measurement (taken over pullover) and add at least 5 cm (2 in) to sleeve length. The front facings should be 6·5 cm (approx $2\frac{1}{2}$ in) wide, if anorak is to be overlapped; 3 cm (approx $1\frac{1}{4}$ in) for a centre front zipper. Lower armhole of pattern by 2·5 cm (1 in) and add 2 cm ($\frac{3}{4}$ in) to both sides of sleeve pattern. Cut pattern off well below child's lower hipline, plus 3·8 cm ($1\frac{1}{2}$ in) for hem. Lengthen, if using jacket pattern.

The easiest plan is to lay coat or jacket pattern on large sheets of paper, going over seam lines with a tracing wheel, marking in the new outlines on the paper, and adding seam allowances. Cut out and pin new pattern together, and try on, adjusting if necessary. Lay quilted material out singly, with wadding on top. Arrange pattern pieces, reversing second halves of front and sleeve. Mark all indications with crayon, and cut out. Cut lining as garment.

For a hood, measure head (*fig 128*), make a pattern from *fig 129*, with lower edges to fit between centre front notches on garment neckline. Add 1 cm ($\frac{3}{8}$ in) for front hem. Cut out hood in quilting and lining, and join seams of both. With right sides facing, stitch hood fronts together, turn to right side, and do a row of top stitching 1·3 cm ($\frac{1}{2}$ in) from fold edge (*figs 130a and b*). Join and press shoulders of garment. Place hood to neckline, right sides together, keeping lining clear. Pin and tack edge, matching notches. Stitch. Turn in neck edges of lining and hem to stitching at neck seam. Work eyelets at hem and in hood for cords.

*Front opening*

For overwrapped opening, apply Velcro, described in chapter 12. For zipped opening, buy the metal open-ended type 5 cm (2 in) shorter than finished front length. Put in by central method (chapter 12), keeping stitching 1 cm ($\frac{3}{8}$ in) from closed seam. If zipper tape seems too narrow, hem its outer edges to seam turnings inside before machining. Join underarm and sleeve seams and set in. Turn up and stitch hems. Make up lining completely. Press turnings 1·5 cm ($\frac{5}{8}$ in) to inside and place inside anorak. Pin folded edges just inside hems, and well clear of zipper at fronts. Slip hem all round, enclosing edges at neck. Make strong neck hanger and attach (chapter 17).

*Cords*

Insert nylon cord in holes, pierced and oversewn at hood and in bottom hem, and thread into 'acorn' beads (from most department stores) and knot ends tightly. A good substitute for these are the tops of small-size toothpaste tubes. Pierce holes in tops with red hot stiletto, and push cord through.

## Anorak with knitted bands at neck, bottom and cuffs

With thick wool and small needles, knit ribbed bands twice finished depth, using an extra strand for several rows where band will turn over. Make bands to fit child – not edges of garment. Make anorak up, except for zipper. Fold neckband in half lengthwise, oversew ends, and turn to right side. Pin each end of band to front notches at neckline, right sides together, stretch band to fit, easing material evenly on to it. Tack and stitch. Apply bottom band in same way. Join sleeve bands into a circle, fold, pin, and stitch to sleeve ends, stretching to fit. Press all turnings towards garment. With this version, zipper should come to within 1·5 cm ($\frac{5}{8}$ in) of band at bottom. Put zip in as above, but hand stitch in at band. Make up and put in lining, stretching bands while inserting pins to take up ease evenly.

## Duffle coats

Here, too, a loose easy fit is essential. Choose a warm, non-fraying wool or wool/synthetic

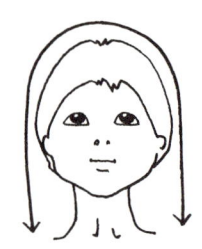

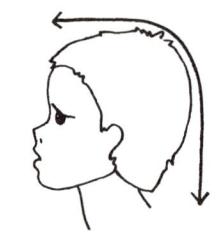

*Fig 128 Where to measure a child's head*

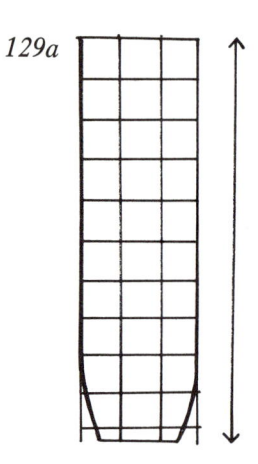

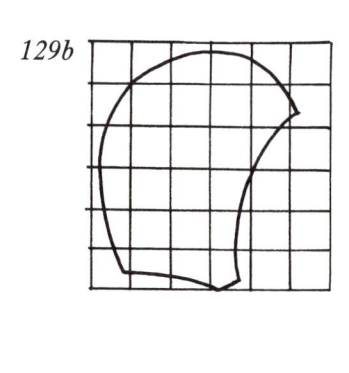

*Figs 129a and b Pattern guide for anorak hood*

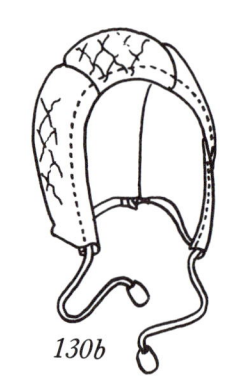

*Fig 130a Anorak hood stitched, before turning right side out*

*Fig 130b Finished anorak hood*

mixture cloth, and a simple coat pattern with set-in or raglan sleeves. These coats are usually unlined, and seams are flat and top stitched. If adapting a coat pattern, lower armhole by 2·5 cm (1 in), adding 1·5 cm ($\frac{5}{8}$ in) to edges of sleeve seam. Also add 1 cm ($\frac{3}{8}$ in) to all seam allowances. Interfacing is required only inside front facings,

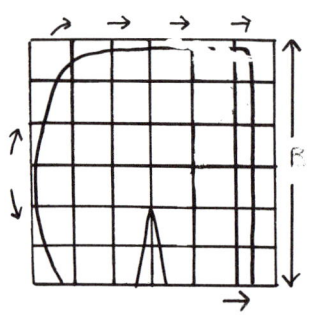

*Fig 131 Pattern guide for shaping duffle coat hood. Squares = 5 cm (2 in) each*

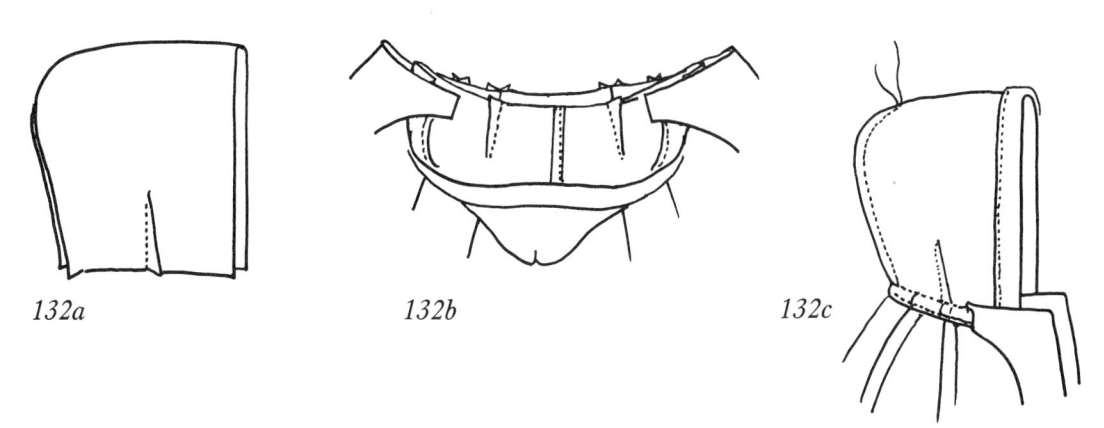

*Figs 132a, b, and c*
*Making a duffle coat hood*

132a

132b

132c

and cut as these. Make hood pattern as shown in *fig 131*, after measuring child as indicated on *fig 128*. Make lower edge to fit between notches at coat neck, allowing 5 cm (2 in) at front. Cut out coat and hood. Stitch shoulder seams, press turnings towards back, and trim underlayer to 6 mm ($\frac{1}{4}$ in). From right side, top stitch 1 cm ($\frac{3}{8}$ in) from join. Make hood (*figs 132a, b, and c*), top stitching as above. Turn facing under, and hem. Place right side of hood to right side of neckline, matching notches. Pin and tack. Fold front facing to outside, taking in front edges of hood. Tack firmly, and stitch entire neckline. Turn facings inside. Layer neck edges, press turnings downwards, and press well. Top stitch. If cloth is very thick, bind neck edges instead. Neaten side seams.

*Pockets*
Make patch pockets, or pockets in side seams, using self material for pocket bags (see chapter 13). Join side seams, make sleeves, and set in. Turnings at armholes are pressed towards sleeves, layered, and top stitched. Bottom and sleeve hems may be machined, if preferred, 1·5 cm ($\frac{5}{8}$ in) from edge. On thick materials, raw edges are zig-zagged first, bound or overcast. Press entire garment.

*Fig 133 How to arrange frogging from cord or braid*

*Fig 134 Finished frogging*

133
134

*Frogging* (figs 133 and 134)
Buy this ready made, or make your own. Get firm round matching or contrasting braid, or thick white nylon cord. Dye this to match, with a cold water dye. Draw out the frogging shape on tissue paper, and arrange cord over the design, making sure that both sides of design have loops crossing in opposite directions. Hold cording in place and sticky tape or tacking. Have buttons at hand, and test central loop for correct size for button to pass through. Arrange paper on coat overwrap, stitch down the cord with tiny back stitches, and tear away paper. Repeat at each fastening position. Sew on buttons or toggles in correct positions with small buttons at back (*fig 135*). Make and apply neck hanger.

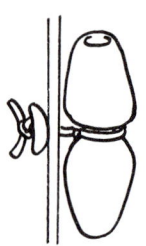

*Fig 135 Toggle secured with a button on the inside*

*Fig 136 Finished anorak and duffle coat*

# 17

# How to get that Tailor-made Look

A child's tailored coat – however small – calls for the same precision, attention to detail, and undercover work as is put into an adult garment. This explains the relatively high cost of children's coats of good quality, and why it is so worthwhile to master the techniques of tailoring and make these yourself.

For a first attempt, choose a straightforward style with collar, revers, pockets, and set-in sleeves – the essential features of tailored garments.

*Materials*
Because of its malleability (especially when damp) and natural crease recovery, pure wool is still the ideal medium for tailoring. Moulding of collars, lapels, and sleeve tops is achieved more easily than with synthetic materials. However, mixtures with a high proportion of wool, eg wool/Terylene or Fortrel, are now popular. Pure wool materials must be pre-shrunk (as described in chapter 7). Interfacing should be a woven type of suitable weight for the material, eg lightweight linen, or synthetic hair canvas; also a finer quality for the back, sleeve ends, and hem. You'll

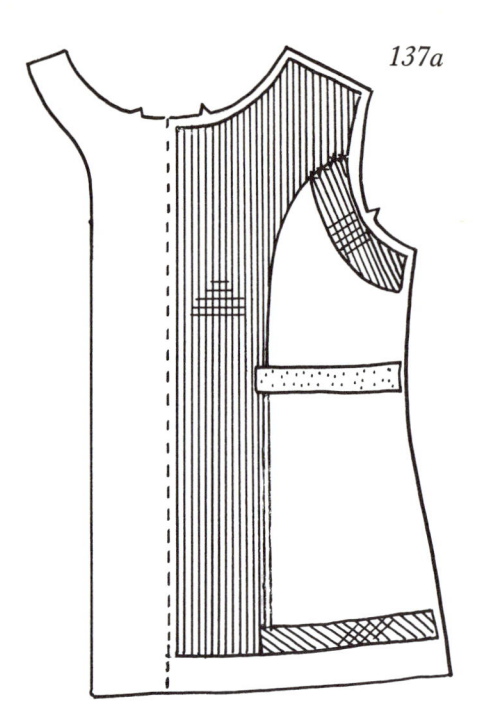

*Figs 137a and b Applying woven and non-woven interfacing to coat*

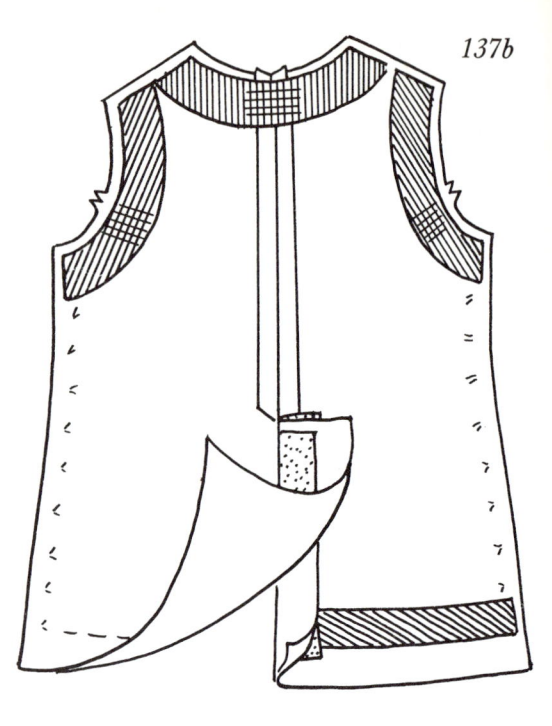

need narrow linen or cotton twill tape for staying. These, too, should be pre-shrunk by soaking in cold water before use.

Modern linings are usually of wholly synthetic yarns, so need not be pre-shrunk. Choose the best possible quality; a poor lining will quickly wear out.

*Applying interfacing (figs 137a and b)*
If no special pattern is given, cut front interfacing from front of garment, curving up to 5 cm (2 in) below front armhole, without hem allowance. A back interfacing, or 'buggy' (*fig 138*) adds shape and stability to a tailored garment. Use thinner interfacing for this, shaping it as shown.

After cutting out and tailor-tacking all pattern indications, run lines of stay stitching along neck, shoulder, and armhole seam line before handling. Lay front pattern over front inter-

*Fig 138 Optional shaped back facing, cut on cross*

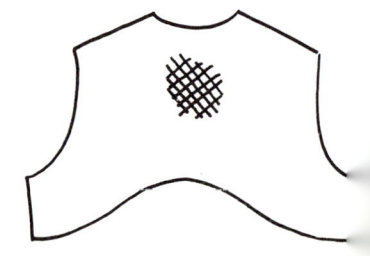

*Fig 139 Tailor's method of making a dart in interfacing*

facing, and again mark in all indications. Make darts in fronts and back of garment, open and press over pad. Stitch centre back seam (if any) and press. Cut darts in interfacing (*fig 139*), and lap over. Trim, and cross stitch edges together. Now lay garment fronts and back on table, right side down, and place interfacings over and tack. Clip off corners on interfacing, diagonally. Apply interfacing at pocket positions (*fig 140*).

Prepare and apply chosen pockets, and make bound buttonholes (chapters 12 and 13) on appropriate front.

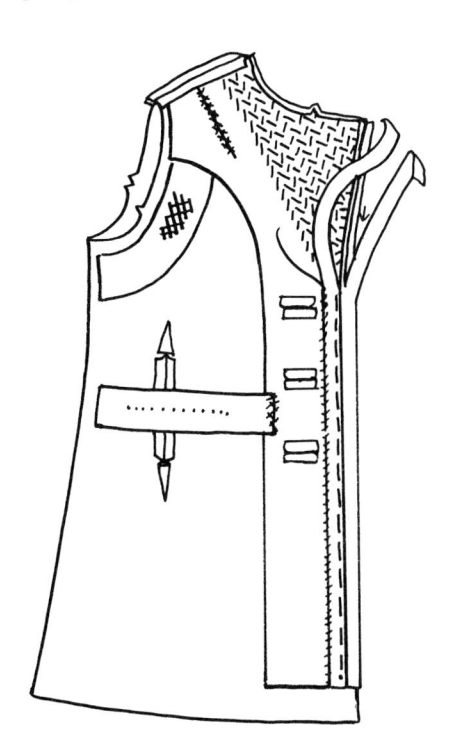

*Fig 140 Preparing the coat front*

*Pad stitching (fig 141)*
Easy – when you know how. On front interfacing, mark the 'roll line', and begin at neck end, holding material in a curve over the left hand. Using a long thread (silk is best), take up small horizontal stitches, and work parallel rows 6 mm

($\frac{1}{4}$ in) apart in alternate directions, building in a permanent roll to within 1·5 cm ($\frac{5}{8}$ in) of outer edge. Cut interfacing away from front edge, and lay tape on firmly – not tightly – catching inner edge to interfacing, as shown. Stitch shoulder seam, easing back edge on to front (unless there's a dart), open, and press turnings apart.

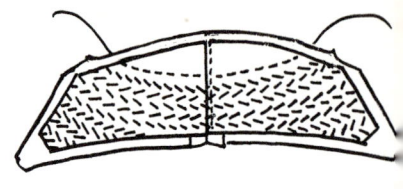

*Fig 141 Pad stitching the collar*

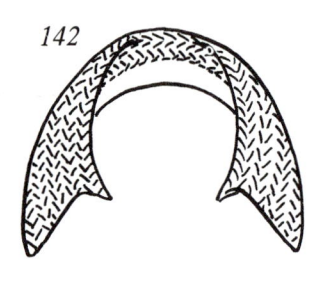

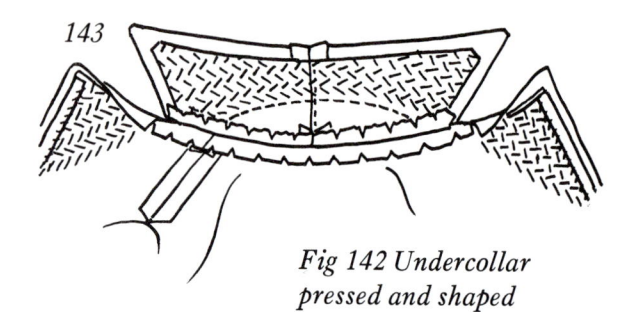

*Fig 142 Undercollar pressed and shaped*

*Fig 143 Attaching the undercollar*

*Fig 144 Attaching the top collar*

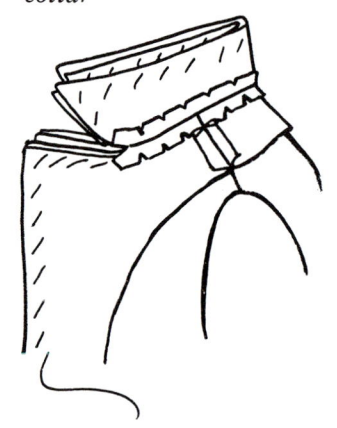

*Collar (figs 141, 142, 143, and 144)*
The success of the collar depends on its undercollar. Join seam in collar interfacing by lapping and cross stitching. Join undercollar seam, trim turnings, and press. Clip corner off interfacing and place to wrong side of undercollar. Fold collar in correct position, and mark fold line with a row of tacking. Starting on fold line, and holding in a curve, work rows of pad stitching towards outer edge, as for lapels. Press folded undercollar over shaped pad or tailor's cushion (see chapter 7).

Clip neckline at 2·5 cm (1 in) intervals, and pin and tack undercollar to coat, matching centre back and all notches. Stitch collar seam to end of seam allowance each end. Clip and open turnings. Pin up side seams, and try coat on child to check fit at neck. Should collar poke forward at back neck, remove coat, put in a double gathering thread at collar fold line and draw up to fit snugly. Tack tape along neckline to maintain correct fit.

*Collar facings*

Join back to front facings, matching notches at collar ends. Clip turnings and press open. Join top collar to facings. With right sides together, match centre back of top collar to centre back of undercollar. Front facings and top collar are cut slightly large to allow for rolling, so ease facing on to undercollar and lapels. Baste facings to coat fronts and stitch, taking in tape. Start at hem, going up, round collar and neck to centre back. Start other side from hem, meeting stitching at centre back. Press all turnings apart, and layer edges. Turn facings inside, and edge tack, rolling seam as follows: towards inside from hem to first buttonhole, and towards outside from buttonhole, round lapels and collar. Use silk thread for this. Press all edges, using shaped pad for collar and lapels. When dry, cut threads at frequent intervals – never pull out long lengths. Press again. Catch stitch facings to interfacing to within 10 cm (4 in) of hem down fronts, and catch neck facings to interfacings.

Finish backs of bound buttonholes (chapter 12). Sew on buttons with long shanks, and put small buttons behind them.

*Sleeves*

Now is the time to set in sleeves, because only when collar and facings have been fitted can exactly correct hang of sleeves be ascertained. Prepare sleeve head, gathering, shrinking, and/or easing to fit armhole (chapter 11). Stitch sleeve seams, easing or darting fullness at underarm seams. Try garment on child, and pin sleeves in, adjusting position so that it hangs in line with the arm. Remove, and baste and stitch sleeves in. Press sleeve top over shaped pad, with turnings towards sleeve. Don't press underarm half or clip turnings.

*Hem and sleeve ends (figs 145 and 146)*
Mark exact fold line for hem with tacking line. Lay a shaped strip of light interfacing 2 cm ($\frac{3}{4}$ in) wider than hem allowance along fold line, catch stitching lower edge to garment. Extend strip on to front interfacing and secure (see chapter 14). Turn up hem, and catch stitch to interfacing only, except at seam turnings. Catch to these. Hem bottom of front facings as shown in *fig 145*. Press hem edge only.

*Lining*
Cut out lining, making any adjustments made to coat or jacket, and tailor tack. Fold in and baste

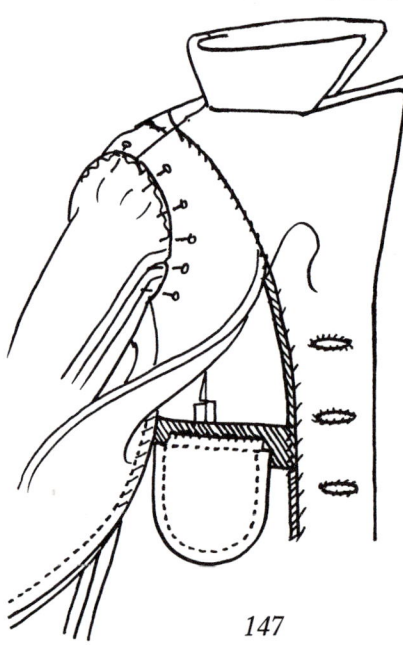

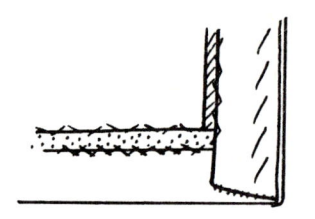

*Fig 145 Finishing the hem*

*Fig 146 Finishing the sleeve end*

*Fig 147 Lining sleeves*

*Fig 148 Stitching in sleeves*

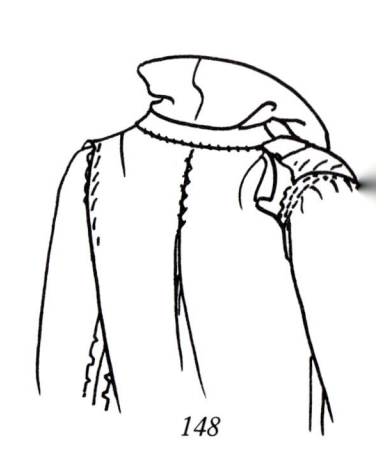

147

148

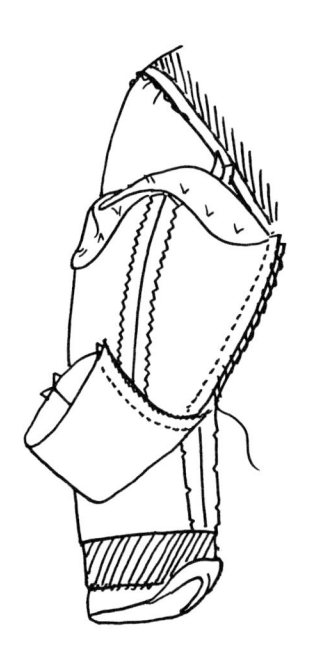

*Fig 149 Putting in sleeve lining*

*Fig 150 Neck hanger*

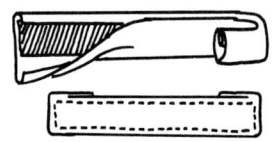

front shoulder darts, and stitch any other darts and side seams. Press side seams, keeping turnings together. Lay garment on table, wrong side uppermost, and place lining body over it, right side on top. Insert pins down centre back line. Fold fronts of lining over back of coat, and baste turnings of lining to coat turnings from 5 cm (2 in) below armhole to 10 cm (4 in) from hem. Baste lining to armholes with long tacks (*fig 147*).

Smooth lining fronts over garment facings, pin and tack including shoulders. Turn in front edges and slip hem to front facings to within 5 cm (2 in) of hemline. Pin back lining over front lining at shoulders. Trim down and clip round neck edges, and fold raw edge down, placing and pinning back lining over back neck facing. Form any surplus in lining into an inverted pleat at centre back. Slip hem lining at neck and shoulders (*fig 148*).

Hem bottom of lining separately, making it 2·5 cm (1 in) shorter than coat. Catch lining to coat turnings at sides with long tacks. Turn up sleeve ends on to interfacing and catch stitch.

Make sleeve linings as sleeve, and press. Turn garment sleeve and lining sleeve to wrong side and place underarm seam of appropriate sleeve lining to garment sleeve seam (*fig 149*). Pin, and tack sleeve turnings together to within 7·5 cm (3 in) of sleeve end. Insert a hand into sleeve lining, grasp sleeve end, and turn through to outside. Slip hem sleeve lining round armhole, arranging fullness into small pleats. Slip hem lining to sleeve ends, lifting slightly to allow extra ease.

Make a neck hanger, enclosing narrow tape, as shown in *fig 150*, and stitch to neck at back of collar with stab stitches.

# 18
# Plaids and Checks

Plaids and checks are always popular for children's skirts, kilts, dresses, shorts, and trews. They always look colourful and smart. Choosing, and making these up, however, calls for great care, and an understanding of the different types of plaids and their limitations if many common pitfalls are to be avoided.

**Patterns**
Choose basically simple styles, with as few seams and as little 'cutting about' as possible, to keep the plaid design unbroken. Note carefully all references to checks and plaids on back of pattern envelope. Where it's specifically stated that a style is unsuitable for these materials, don't risk disaster. Choose another. Where mentioned that extra material will be needed for plaids etc, amounts will be determined by the size of the

plaid and its repeat and by garment and number of pleats (if any). Average amounts are 50 cm ($\frac{1}{2}$ yd) to 60 cm ($\frac{5}{8}$ yd) for medium to large checks. The larger the plaid or check the more material you'll need. Small checks are more suitable for young children. The plaid design should always be kept in proportion to the size of the child.

**Types of plaid**

1 *Balanced plaids* have the colours or bars repeated in the same sequence on both sides of main blocks, both on crosswise and lengthwise threads. This type is the easiest and most economical to cut, and looks just as effective as this next type.

2 *Unbalanced plaids* make for wasteful cutting out. Here, not always detected at first glance, the design of blocks and bars is repeated in the same sequence either side of dominant blocks lengthwise, crosswise, or both. Always examine this type to see whether there's a right and a wrong side. If both sides are identical, laying up will be more economical. If not, it will be impossible to match opposite halves of garments.

When planning patterns on plaids and checks, avoid placing main pieces so as to break up main block. Keep these to the centre, or equally either side. Decide where dominant block is to come on main pieces, and mark these on edges of corresponding patterns, adjusting other pieces so that crosswise blocks and bars come in identical positions on matching seam lines. Always remember to make allowance for the front wrapover so design isn't broken up when the garment is fastened.

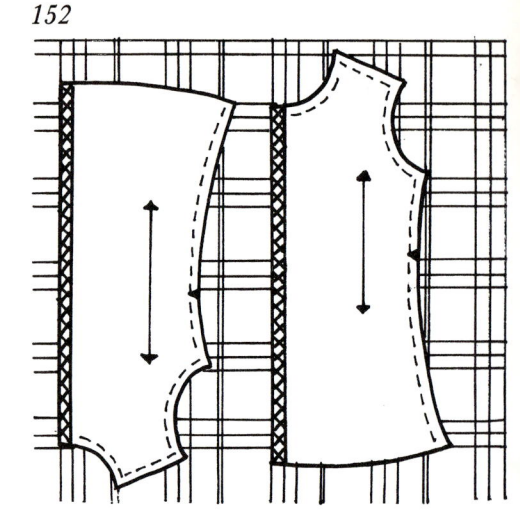

*Fig 151 Unbalanced plaid, lengthwise only*

*Fig 152 Unbalanced plaid, crosswise only*

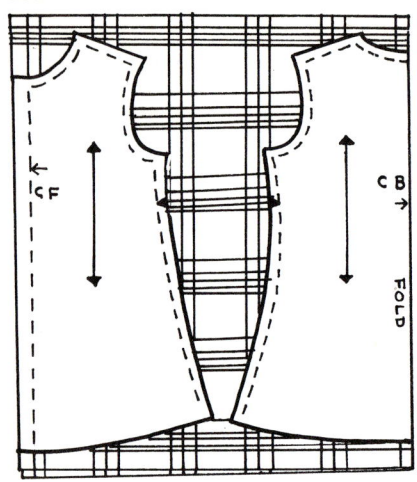

**Cutting out plaid**

*Cutting unbalanced plaids*

*Uneven lengthwise only (fig 151)*
Arrange pieces so that plaids are balanced either side of dominant block. Place a centre fold to middle of dominant block. Then follow the 'with nap' layout on pattern instruction sheet.

*Uneven crosswise only (fig 152)*
Cut on single material. Fronts and backs must have a centre seam. Arrange these as shown, allowing turnings where marked 'fold' on pattern beyond centre of dominant block. For opposite halves, reverse the pieces, also placing on material the opposite way up to ensure balance.

*Unbalanced plaid in both directions (fig 153)*
Choose material with no right or wrong side. Open material singly, arranging centre seam to come halfway across a dominant block. If material is marked 'fold', add 1·5 cm ($\frac{5}{8}$ in) turnings.

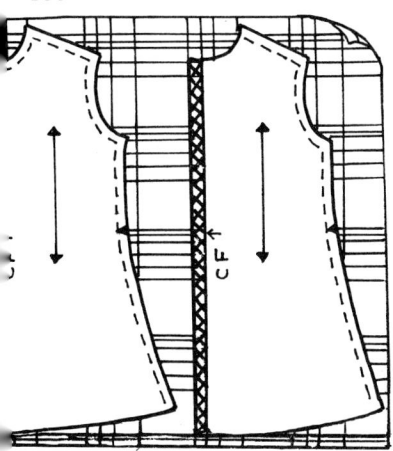

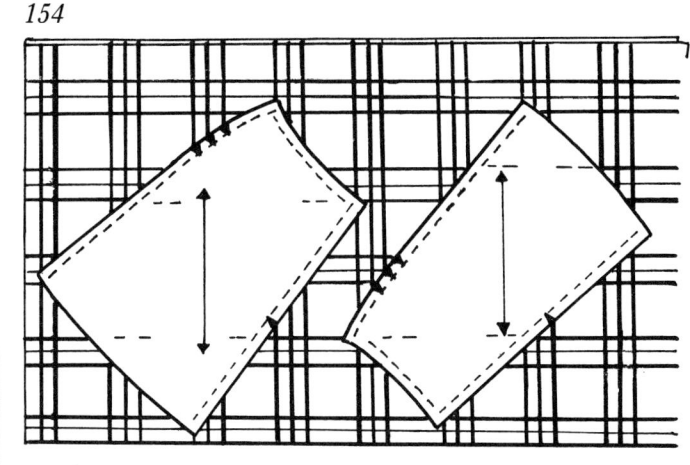

*Fig 153 Unbalanced plaid in both directions*

*Fig 154 Arranging pattern pieces crosswise on plaid*

Cut out one main piece, leave pattern pinned to it, then place it elsewhere on an identical plaid arrangement, matching lengthwise and crosswise bars. Repeat with opposite halves of all pieces. When making up, reverse halves are placed against outside pieces to achieve balanced opposites.

*Cutting plaids and checks on the cross (fig 154)*
Girls' plaid or check skirts are often cut on the cross to give a chevron effect. Choose an even, balanced design to save headaches! If material is identical on both sides, fold and pin selvedges as described. Place skirt back on true cross, mark where dominant bars or checks come on the pattern, and cut out. With pattern still pinned, place it on to skirt front, and mark off checks etc to correspond. Then cut out front.

When laying up plaids and checks, decide where dominant block is to come on all main pieces, marking these on edges of patterns. Adjust other pieces so that all crosswise blocks and bars come in identical positions on matching seam lines.

## Making up plaid

*Tacking seamlines*
To ensure absolutely accurate matching up, fold under one seam edge 1·5 cm ($\frac{5}{8}$ in), crease and lap this over corresponding edge, pinning edges at each bar with pins at right angles. Insert needle into fold edge and under layer, taking horizontal stitches 6 mm ($\frac{1}{4}$ in) long through fold and under layer.

*Pockets in plaid etc*
The design should match exactly, but small checks look effective if cut on the cross. Avoid using large plaids for small areas, eg collars, cuffs etc.

*Darts in plaids and checks*
Where darts come in front, match bars and checks from hem up to dart. Distortion above dart is inevitable. Make neck and elbow darts, matching crosswise bars only.

## Simplified tartan kilt (*fig 155*)

Two widths of 140 cm (54–56 in) balanced plaid material will make a kilt for any hip measurement up to 75 cm (30 in), without a pattern. To actual hip measurement add 7·5 cm (3 in) for ease. When calculating pleats, allow 7·5 cm (3 in) for each 2·5 cm (1 in) more or less required to obtain the correct measurement. To find the amount required, measure child from waist to hem, double this, and add 40 cm (16 in) for hem, waistband, and fringing.

    Choose lightweight wool, wool/Terylene or wool/Fortrel, because material must withstand steam pressing. If all-wool, then pre-shrink (chapter 7). Choose a balanced plaid.

*Fig 155 Simplified tartan kilt*

*Fig 156 Pleating under section*

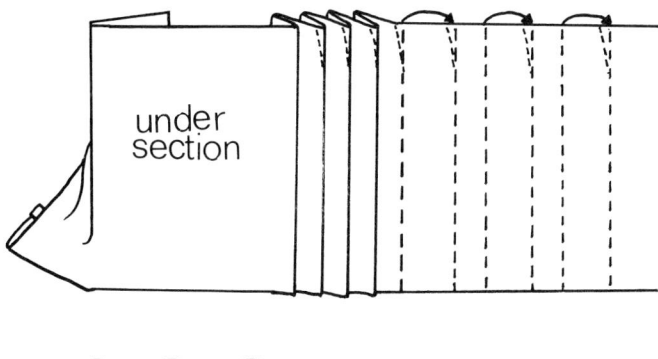

*Fig 157 Pleating upper section*

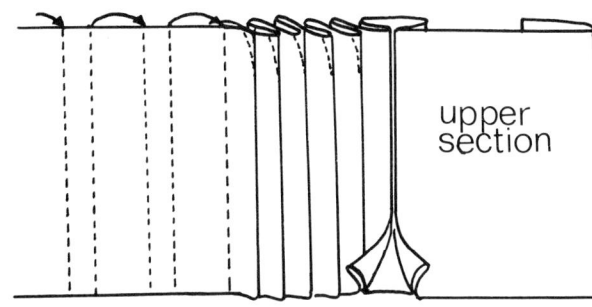

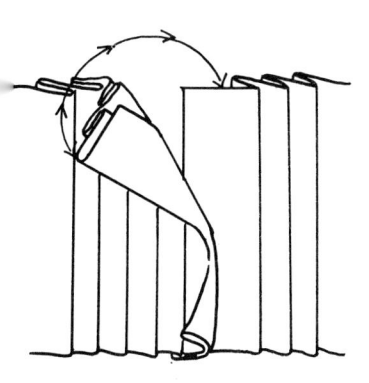

*Fig 158 Arrangement at join*

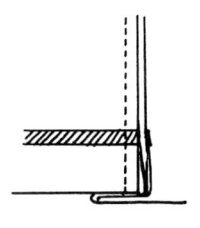

*Fig 159 Inside of join*

Fold material in half along (centre) of a bar, and cut exactly along a thread. At bottom of both pieces, cut off 20·5 cm (8 in). Turn up hem, tack, and press.

*Pleating under section (fig 156)*
Lay material on table, right side up, and working from the left mark off 28 cm (11 in) for facing and under panel, and tack lines. Crease, pin, and tack pleats, starting 7·5 cm (3 in) down from waist edge, as shown.

*Pleating upper section (fig 157)*
Working from right, measure off 28 cm (11 in) for panel and facing, and tack. Crease on inner line and form 2·5 cm (1 in) inverted pleat. Working towards left, crease, pin, and tack all pleats (folds towards right). Tack sections together, forming a complete pleat, with join coming inside crease. At waist edge, roll pleats under 6

139

mm (¼ in), bringing crease in line with under fold of next pleat, as shown. Tack pleats from waist to 7·5 cm (3 in) down. Try kilt on, overwrapping panels, facings folded under. The tacked pleats should hang straight, without straining apart. Adjust by increasing or reducing at side join by amounts mentioned. Stitch side join, and neaten facing edges (*figs 158 and 159*).

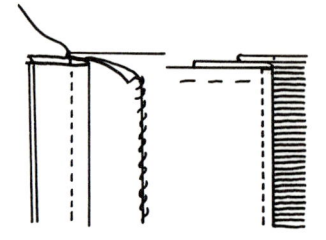

*Fig 160 Attaching fringing*

*Fringing (fig 160)*
Cut a strip 7·5 cm (3 in) wide and length of skirt, fold lengthwise, and place fold 6 mm (¼ in) behind fold edge of upper panel. Tack and edge stitch from outside. Fringe out projecting edges.

*Tab on waistband (figs 161a, b, and c)*
Make a tab as shown. Edge stitch and press. Cut waistband 7·5 cm (3 in) wide, to fit top of kilt. Fold lengthwise (right side inside). Place raw edge of tab to end of band, as shown. Stitch across ends of band, turn, and press. Pin end with tab to end of front panel, right sides together. Tack inner edge of band to waist edge, and stitch. Turn band inside, fold raw edge under and slip hem to machine stitches. For a closer fit at back waist, insert wide elastic inside waistband from panel to side join. Attach a suitable buckle to waistband in line with inverted pleat on upper panel. Finish with kilt pin.

    For younger children, crossed straps may be made and attached to waistband to hold kilt up. For boys, make as for girl but with panels reversed.

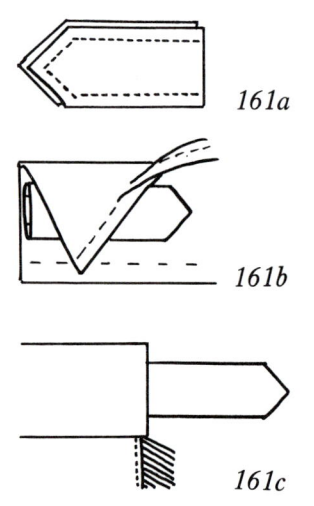

*161a*

*161b*

*161c*

*Figs 161a, b, and c Stages in making a tab*

# 19
# Ideas for Party Clothes

Party clothes aren't meant to last for more than a season or two. Originality and gaiety are of first importance. And by planning one or two outfits with separates – frilly blouses (for boys), long dresses worn over a well fitting slip, often with a pretty top over (for girls), it's possible to ring the changes far more often.

Nowadays, quite small girls enjoy wearing long party dresses. Strangely, too, boys are beginning to make fewer objections to being 'dressed up' for those special occasions. The plain white shirt and dark shorts or 'longs' – once their only concession – have given place to velvet trews or knickerbockers, and Spanish-type frilled shirts, all of which give plenty of scope to the imaginative dressmaker.

**Ideas for girls**
Full skirts, frilled hems, and lace edgings with fitting bodice, often in a dark colour, will suit both chubby and thin children. Highly popular for festive occasions – and even for everyday wear – is the Victorian-type pinafore worn over a classic long-sleeved dress (*fig 162*). Calf-length dresses with a pinafore on top, worn over frilly bloomers which peep out below in Alice in

*Fig 162 Classic dress*

Wonderland style, look enchanting on younger girls.

Making party outfits certainly presents the perfect opportunity to use up those odd remnants, too small to make an entire garment. By combining two or more materials of different types and colours, it's easy to create attractive and original results.

For most styles the mainstay is a plain dress, with long, fairly close fitting sleeves which may be smoothly rounded or gathered at the sleeve head. The bodice will be fitted at rather higher than natural waist level, and the skirt flared or slightly gathered on to the bodice. Plenty of patterns are available on these simple lines.

*Fig 163a Simple pinafore*

*Fig 163b Pinafore with double yoke*

*Pinafores (figs 163a and b)*
Choose any crisp – preferably crease-resistant – material. Polycottons are ideal. If in white, trim the neck and armholes with broderie anglaise or coarse lace. It's simple to make a pattern from a plain dress or simple smock. A square necked yoke with skirt gathered on is highly practical and very comfortable. The pinafore may be opened at the front or back, and fastened with buttons or tied with self tapes.

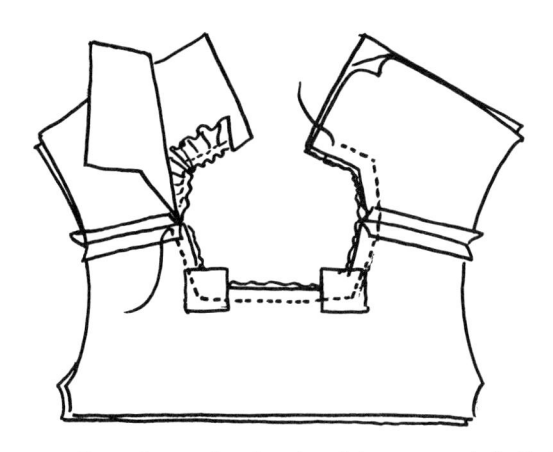

*Fig 164 Applying broderie anglaise between layers of yoke*

*Fig 165 Adapting a trousers pattern for bloomers*

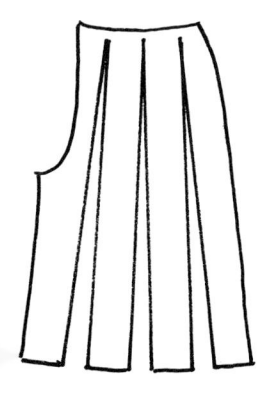

Cut the yoke in double material. Join shoulder seams. If trimming with broderie anglaise (*fig 164*), gather this up – not too much – to fit the neckline with two rows of machining and pin to neckline edge of one layer of yoke, right sides together. Tack, and remove pins. Place second layer on top. Apply small squares of non-woven interfacing at each corner to strengthen. Stitch on seam line, clip into corner, trim edges, and turn to right side. Neaten ends of trim with a tiny hand-rolled hem.

Gather top of skirt to fit yoke, and set edge between layers as follows: place skirt edge, right sides together, to top layer of yoke, pin, and stitch. Turn under and slip hem-free edge of yoke to back of machine stitches. Stitch up side seams, and apply trimming to outside of arm-holes. Fold turning to inside and face with cross-way binding.

If you like, these popular pinafores can have long, loose sleeves, with lace-trimmed neck and sleeve ends. Alternatively, frilly epaulettes look most attractive.

*Bloomers*
A jeans or trouser pattern can be adapted for these (*fig 165*). To find the correct length, try the

*Fig 166 Leg bands for bloomers*

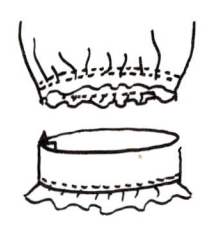

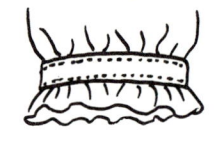

finished overdress on the child, and take the measurement from hemline to floor. Remove dress, place the trouser pattern against the child, and mark pattern leg approximately 2·5 cm (1 in) below hem. Place pattern pieces on a large sheet of paper, and mark and slash, increasing finished width of leg about half as much again. Draw round new outline, and cut pieces out. Cut out and make up bloomers, using a French seam. Make a small slot at waist for elastic. Run two rows of gathers along bottom of legs, using largest machine stitch. Cut two bands, twice required width, plus turnings to fit child's leg quite loosely. Join each band into a circle, and draw up legs of bloomers to fit. Apply broderie anglaise or self frills to one edge of two of the bands (*fig 166*). Apply other edge to bloomer legs and stitch. Back on inside with other pair of bands. For lace trim, cut band double, apply to bloomers on right side, turn free end to inside, fold under, and slip hem. Sew lace on fold edge.

*Foundation slip*
A party dress, long or short, always looks so much better if worn over a foundation slip. Once more, make use of the bodice pattern of a dress, either a one-piece, by extending and flaring out the side seams from waist level to length desired, or by making a separate skirt and bodice. But here, make sure that waist seam coincides exactly with that of dress. Material for a slip should be

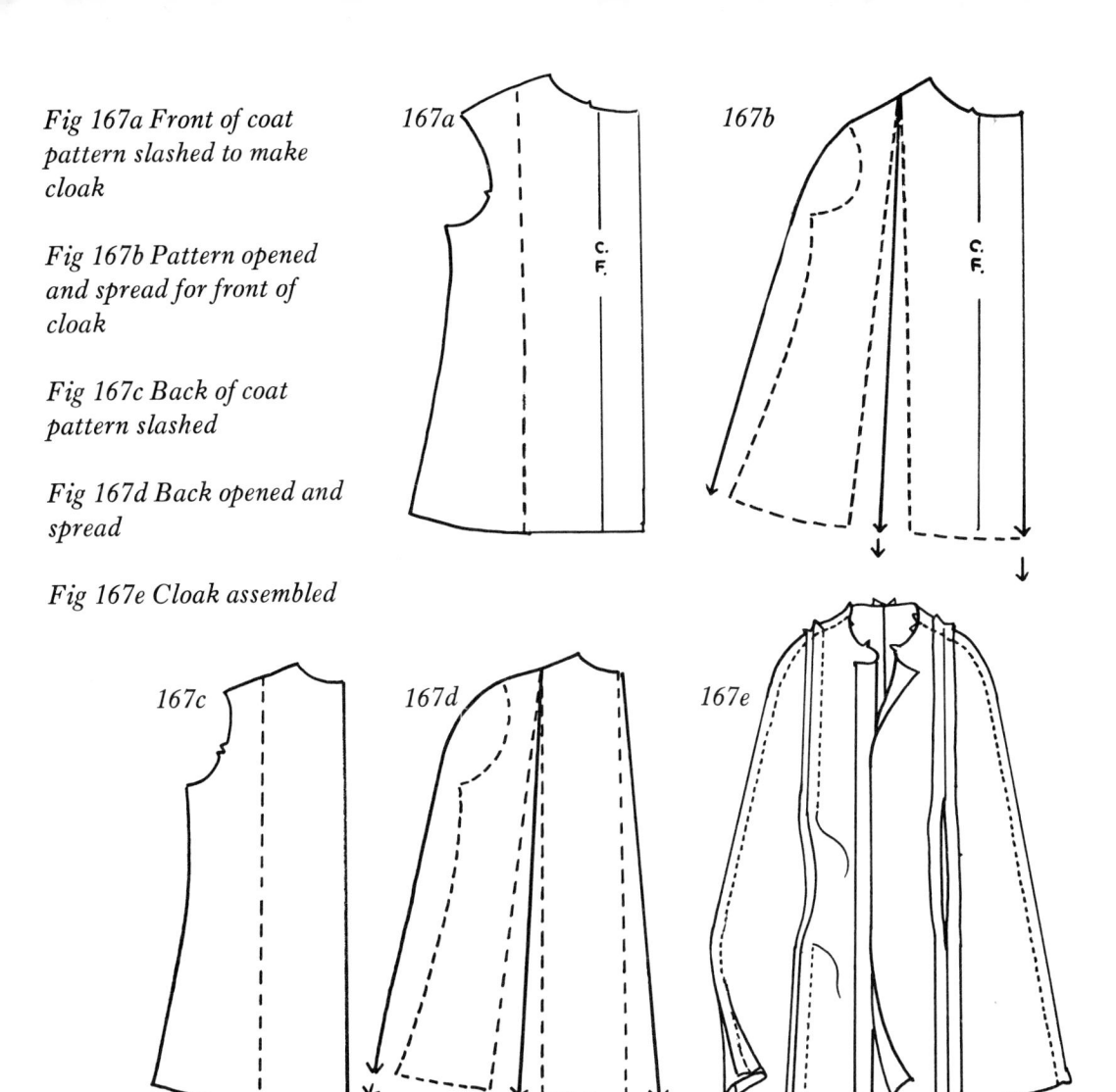

*Fig 167a Front of coat pattern slashed to make cloak*

*Fig 167b Pattern opened and spread for front of cloak*

*Fig 167c Back of coat pattern slashed*

*Fig 167d Back opened and spread*

*Fig 167e Cloak assembled*

smooth, firmly woven, and in a colour that won't shadow through thin materials. Make the hem 5 cm (2 in) shorter than hem of dress. Scoop out at neck and shoulders, bind edges with self material, and trim with lace.

### Party cloak (figs 167a–k)

These days, a cloak is a 'must' to wear over long dresses. Make one in velvet, or a wool mixture, and line with any bright contrasting material.

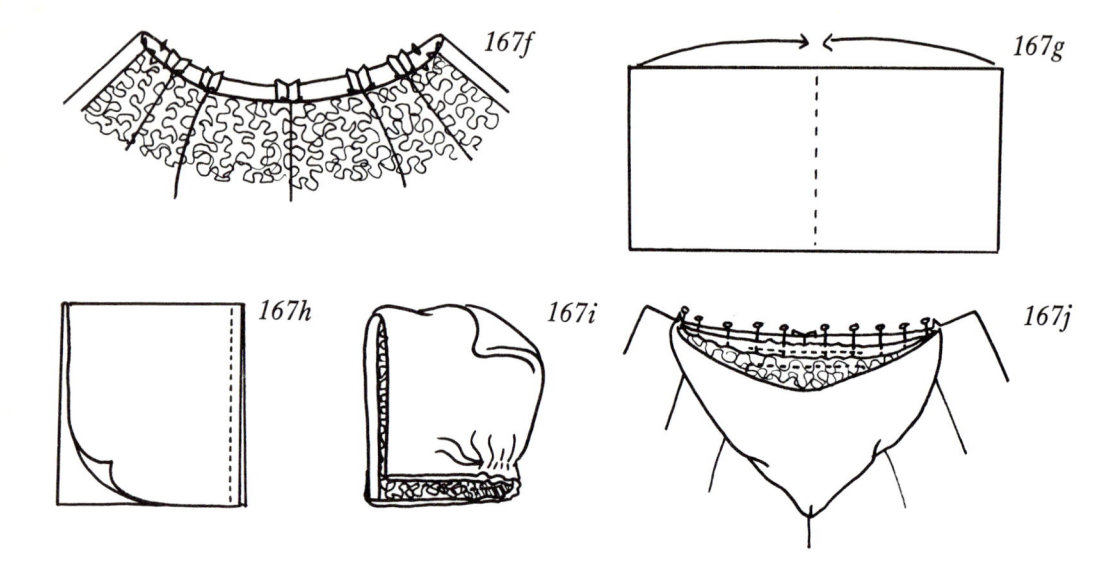

Save on patterns again by adapting the front and back of a coat or dress pattern. A full-length cloak should be fairly wide and loose, but fitting smoothly over the shoulders. Measure the child from nape of neck to required finished length, and from side of neck over shoulder to same distance from floor. *Front pattern.* Draw a line from centre of shoulder to hem, parallel with front edge, and cut on line. Lay pieces on a very large sheet of paper. Meet sections at shoulder and spread to 7·5 cm–15 cm (3–6 in) at hemline, and pin down. Draw round neck and shoulders, extending lines down and out to new length, as shown. Add 7·5 cm (3 in) facings at front. If using dress pattern, add 5 cm (2 in) additionally for wrapover. Cut out, adding turnings to panel seams. *Back pattern.* Mark and slash pattern, as for front. *Hood.* Make as shown. Lower line is cape neck measure, plus 7·5 cm (3 in). Depth is half child's head measure taken from front neck to top of head, adding 7·5 cm (3 in) for facing.

Plan a trial layout on newspaper to find amount of material needed, and sketch. (If using

*Fig 167f Inside of lined cloak*

*Fig 167g Guide for cutting hood*

*Fig 167h Hood stitched*

*Fig 167i Hood made up and lined*

*Fig 167j Hood pinned to neck of cloak (lining edge free)*

velvet, all pieces must go same way.) Cut out cloak and hood in chosen material and lining, minus 5 cm (2 in) on front of hood in lining, and 2·5 cm (1 in) on cloak front in lining only. Join seams in material and lining, leaving open between notches in front panels. With right sides inside join material to lining down fronts to within 5 cm (2 in) of hem. Turn edges inwards at openings, and slip hem together. Join back seam in hood and lining, and place front edges of both together, right sides inside, stitch, turn, and press lightly. Gather back neck of hood and lining separately, and place neck edge of hood to neck of cloak, right sides together between front notches, leaving lining edge free. Tack and stitch. Turn under and hem lining to neck of cloak. Interface hem (see chapter 14) and slip hem lining to cloak hem, making lining 2·5 cm (1 in) shorter. Fasten with frogging, or with button and loop at neck.

*Fig 167k Finished cloak*

*Fig 168 Frills on a plain shirt, worn with knicker-bockers*

**Ideas for boys**
Remnants of furnishing velvet are ideal for making trousers for party wear. It's tougher and less easily marked than velvets sold for clothing, too. Make the trousers as described in chapter 15. Pressing must be kept to an absolute minimum, however (see chapter 7), but a permanent crease can be put in by edge stitching down centre front and back of trousers.

*Victorian-type velvet knickerbockers (fig 168)*
These are now appearing for small boys. Here, too, a well-fitting jeans or trousers pattern can be utilized. Shorten the leg of the pattern to just below the knee, and flare out the outer and inner seams slightly to allow for gathering or easing on to the leg bands. Take the measurement round the child's leg below the knee fairly loosely. Cut two bands (*fig 169*) twice the required width, plus turnings of the length required, and

*Fig 169 Band for knickerbockers*

5 cm (2 in) for a pointed extension. Make up as for trousers, leaving side seam open for 5 cm (2 in) at hem. Face openings on inside. Fold bands lengthwise and stitch as shown. Ease or gather legs on to one edge of bands as far as extension. Turn free edge of band under and slip hem on inside. Work a buttonhole on pointed end and sew button on underside. (If you prefer, fasten with a large press stud instead.)

*Spanish-style shirt (fig 170)*
The addition of self frilling on either side of a plain front opening shirt transforms the everyday item into something special. But for a more elaborate version, use a plain dress pattern, adding facing allowances at the back. Make a stand-up collar (chapter 10) cut on the true cross, with back fastening. Apply two or more rows of frilled lace down the front, and substitute lace frills for the usual shirt cuffs. Add a tape casing at sleeve ends on inside, and insert elastic to fit the wrist.

*Fig 170 Spanish-style shirt*

# 20
# Altering and Adapting Children's Clothes

Nowadays, even very young children have definite ideas about what they like or don't like to wear. Obvious hand-downs are often, understandably, resented by younger brothers and sisters. But for the mother with imagination, adapting, combining, and re-styling outgrown (but not outworn) clothing offers creative possibilities and tremendous savings.

It's a good idea to turn out and go through all outgrown clothes at one go, because, often, unlikely items can be happily partnered to make an entirely new garment.

First, make sure that the material of all garments to be used is sound, with no pulled threads, darns, ineradicable marks, worn, or faded parts. Only combine materials which are compatible in composition, and which require similar treatment in laundering and ironing, eg not linen, which needs a high temperature, with nylon, which has a low melting point!

Test out zippers before re-use, discarding any which stick, have broken sliders, missing teeth, or worn tapes.

**Enlarging and lengthening**

Try the garment on the child, and see exactly where the strain comes – armholes, neck, waist, or hips. Decide how much longer and wider it should be. Here are some suggestions:

*Fig 171 Enlarging a garment with contrasting bands*

1 Replace a shabby and too tight front fastening with a wider band of contrasting material (*fig 171*) down the front – and at the waist, if too short. Unpick waist seam (if any), and cut off at fronts just beyond buttonholes. Let in material at waist as required, and join on new front band and facings. Apply new fastenings.

*Fig 172 Making a skirt from a too tight dress*

2 Dress with too tight bodice and armhole? (*fig 172*). Cut off bodice at 5 cm (2 in) below armhole. Try skirt part on child, and fit waist at new level. Make a waistband from bodice or sleeve. Or make new bodice and short sleeves from skirt of a too small dress.

3  Make gay boleros, jerkins, and waistcoats (*fig 173*) for boy or girl from best parts of thicker dresses, coats, and jackets. Trim with bright braid or fringing.

4  Use the skirts of outgrown knitted garments to make sleeves and roll collar for another garment in plain material, adding a let-in knit waistband to lengthen (*fig 174*). Incorporate the knitted edge at original hem into collar and sleeve edges – to look professional.

*Fig 173 Making a jerkin from a jacket*

*Fig 174 Lengthening with knitted inset waist, finished with matching collar and cuffs*

5  Adding knitted bands to sleeve ends and hem of too short anoraks (*fig 175*) will add a year or two of extra life.

*Fig 175 Adding knitted band and cuffs to anorak*

*Fig 176 Hats made from a fake fur coat*

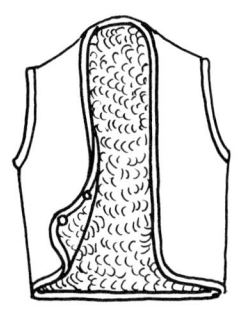

*Fig 177 Detachable interlining*

6 Hang on to the baby's or toddler's furry coats and jackets. Cut these up for trims down fronts of coats, making cosy hats and warm winter mitts (*fig 176*). A fluffy little Acrilan coat, unpicked, can make a warm, detachable interlining for a child's raincoat (*fig 177*). Piece it where necessary, because joins won't show. Make a simple pattern from the child's coat, or a waistcoat pattern, and cut a lining the same, if liked. Bind all edges and sew snap fasteners (no 3 or 4) at equal intervals on edges of lining, with corresponding halves on appropriate positions on coat. Place the finished lining inside coat, spread out flat, and mark positions accurately on both.

7 Make a plain, one-piece dress into a useful tabard (*fig 178*), using the centre part of sleeves to make ties at sides, or straps buttoned on with big, bright buttons.

*Fig 178 Making a tabard from a dress*

8 Torn or worn patch or slot pockets needn't mean discarding a garment. Unpick pockets and replace with larger ones in contrasting material, perhaps adding a new collar or front band to match.

9 Make colourful sun outfits from outgrown gingham and print dresses (*figs 179 and 180*). Separate skirt from bodice; cut off 7·5 cm (3 in) from skirt waist. Make a side opening in skirt (continuous lap, described in chapter 12) and gather top to fit child's waist. Make waistband from piece cut off, gather skirt on band. Cut off bottom of bodice to 7·5 cm (3 in) below armhole. Cut off sleeves, and use to make frill for bottom of bodice. Lower armhole and bind armhole and neck (*fig 180*) with crossway strips cut from sleeves, or purchased binding. A too tight dress in thicker material will make a skirt. Cut off below armholes, and use to make a shaped hip yoke. Try out on child, and attach yoke to skirt of dress. Line, and top stitch.

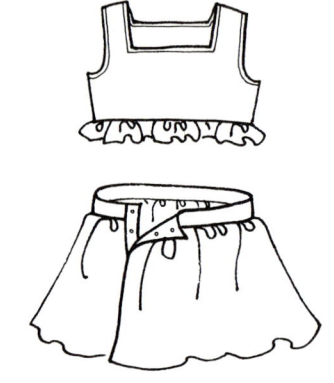

*Fig 179 Two-piece outfit for summer*

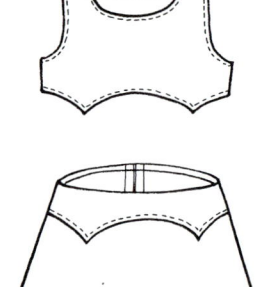

*Fig 180 Two-piece outfit in thicker material*

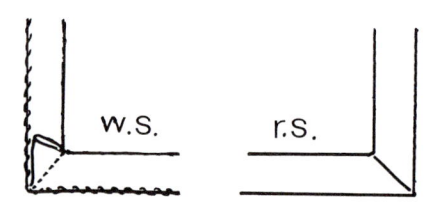

*Fig 181 Binding on square neck*

10 Summer dresses can be converted into attractive 'angel tops' by cutting off at waist level, and adding a wide, frilled, and lace-trimmed peplum from skirt material, with frilled epaulettes to match.

11 Turn outgrown coats into smart jerkins or long waistcoats, by removing sleeves and lowering armholes. Cut armhole facings from sleeve material, or bind with wide wool braid.

*Fig 182 Party shirt from a summer dress*

12 Use an older sister's outgrown summer dress to make a smart party shirt for a little brother (*fig 182*).

*Fig 183 Revitalizing an old blazer*

13 Revitalize a shabby blazer (*fig 183*) by cutting off collar and lapels, making a deep V-line at front 2·5 cm (1 in) above top button. Bind all edges, remove pockets, turn material to wrong side, and bind pockets with braid. Replace in same positions. If the collar and lapels are not worn, just bind them with braid as they are.

14 Trousers and dungarees are difficult to enlarge, but if not too tight, and merely short, the addition of contrasting turn-ups and patch pockets will give longer wear (*fig 184*).

15 Patch dungarees with any strong contrasting material in odd shapes (*fig 185*). Edges may be zig-zagged or turned in and edge stitched. Be sure that patches are considerably larger than the hole or tear, or the material will soon break away. To strengthen thin places, machine a wide strip of material inside front knee area, taken from seam to seam, before applying patch outside.

*Fig 184 Adding contrasting turn-ups and patch pockets to trousers*

## Cut-downs

Using the best parts of adult clothing to make clothes for children presents no special problems. Unpicking takes time, but in money saved most projects are well worthwhile. First, unpick the whole garment – don't be tempted merely to cut around seams. It takes more material than one expects, when cutting out entirely different shapes from irregular pieces! Always wash or dry clean the unpicked pieces before using. Re-use buttons etc only if perfectly sound. Many wool cloths can be made up on the reverse side, where colours will be fresh and new looking. Use new interfacings, since these have usually become limp, with distorted weave.

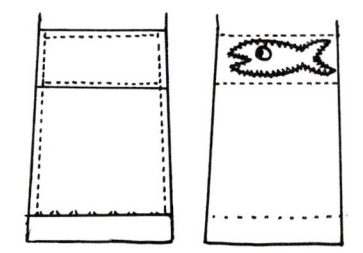

*Fig 185 Decorative patches for worn knees*

# Index

Adapting patterns, 31–8
  blouse, 33
  cape, 36
  collar, 36
  dress, 31–4
  jeans, 35–6
  jerkin, 34
  sleeve, 36
  tabard, 34
  toddler's, 36–8
  trouser, 35–6
  tunic, 34
  waistcoat, 34

Adjusting patterns, 22–30
  accommodating high, round tummy, 24–5
  enlarging tight neckline, 26
  for height, 23
  for narrow shoulders, 27–8
  for sloping shoulders, 27–8
  jeans, 28–30
  sleeve, 23
  taking in loose neckline, 27
  trousers, 28–30

Altering clothes, 150–6
  boy's, 155–6
  cut-downs, 156
  enlarging and lengthening, 151–6
  general ideas, 150, 152–6

Anoraks, 121–3
  adapting pattern, 121
  cords, 123
  front opening, 122
  lengthening with knitted bands, 123
  preparation, 122

Apron, 116

Assembling a garment, 52–9
  dressmaking paper, 54
  marking with crayon or chalk, 53
  seams, 55–6
  tailor tacking, 52–3
  thread outlining, 54
  tracing wheel, 54

Blazer binding, 155

Bloomers, 143–4

Bodkin, 43

Buttonholes, 100–2
  fabric loops, 102
  plain bound, 101–2
  preparation, 100–2
  worked, 101

Capes, 36

Checks, plaids and, 134–40

Cloak for party, 145–7

Coats, 121–6, 127–33

Collars, 82–6
  basic hints, 82–3
  fancy, 86
  finished, 84
  flat, 83–4

157

Collars, (contd)
    Peter Pan, 82–4
    raised at back, 85
    straight, 85

Coverall from raincoat, 116

Cuffs, 92–4
    crossway facing, 94
    elastic, 94
    growth allowance, 17–18
    without opening, 93
    zipped sleeve opening, 93

Cut-downs, 156

Cutting board, 45

Cutting out, 50–1

Dart tucks, 73

Darts, 66, 71–3
    double-ended, 72–3
    interfacing, 80–1
    pressing, 63
    seam, 72

Dress patterns, 31–4
    adapting, 31–4
    bodice, 32
    flared skirt, 32
    high yoke, 32
    pleated skirt, 33
    princess-line, 34

Dressmaker's paper, 44, 54

Duffle coat, 123–6
    adapting pattern, 123–4
    frogging, 126
    making hood, 125
    pockets, 125

Dungarees for toddlers, 117–18
    measuring, 15–17
    patching, 156

Elasticating, 70

Equipment, 39–46

Fastenings, 95–103
    buttonholes, 100–2
    fabric loops, 102
    faced, 98–9
    fly-front, 99–100
    frogging, 126
    front, 18
    hooks and eyes, 103

    press studs, 103
    toggles, 126
    Velcro, 100
    zippers, 95–8

Gathering, 66–8
    machine-made, 67–8

Growth allowance, 37–8

Hats, 153

Hem marker, 45

Hems, 109–14
    blouse, 114
    curved, 113
    even, 109–110
    faced, 111–12
    general hints, 110
    hand-rolled, 111
    interfaced, 114
    jersey, 112–13
    seam bound, 111
    straight, 110–11
    tailor's, 112
    top stitched, 114
    with pleat, 113

Hooks and eyes, 103

Informal clothes, 115–20
    apron, 116
    coverall from raincoat, 116
    dirndl skirt, 116–17
    general hints, 115
    jeans, 118–20
    toddler's dungarees, 117–18
    towel turnabouts, 115–16
    trousers, 118–20

Interfacings, 76–81, 83
    choice, 77–8
    collar, 80
    cutting, 51
    darts, 80–1
    function, 77
    general hints, 78–9
    hem, 114
    iron-on, 81
    non-woven, 77–9
    pocket, 79
    types, 76–7

Jeans, 35–6, 118–20
    adapting pattern, 35–6
    adjusting, 28

fitting, 28–9
measuring, 15–17
older boy's, 118–20

Jerkins, 152, 155
adapting pattern, 34

Kilt, 138–40

Knickerbockers, 148–9

Marking, 51, 53–4

Materials, 18–20
plaids and checks, 134–40
preparation, 48
suitable choice, 18–20
synthetic, 19

Measurements, 13–17, 109–10
general principles, 14
hemline, 109–10
keeping records, 13–14
pattern sizing, 20–1
where to measure, 15–17

Needles, 40–1

Necklines, adjusting, 26–7

Openings, 95–103
faced, 98
measuring, 95

Party clothes, 141–9
bloomers, 143–4
cloak, 145–7
foundation slip, 144–5
Spanish-style shirts, 149
Victorian-style knickerbockers, 148–9

Pattern reading, 47–8
sizing, 20–21

Patterns, adapting, 31–8
adjusting, 22–30
for reference, 30

Pins, 41

Plaids and checks, 134–40
cutting out, 136–40
making-up, 138
patterns, 134–5
simplified kilt, 138–40
types, 135

Pleats, 74–5
accordion, 74

backed, 75
box, 74
inverted, 74
joining, 74
knife, 74
panel seam, 74
sunray, 74

Pockets, 104–8
belt, 108
bound, 104, 106–7
duffle coat, 125
inset, 104, 106
on woven cloth, 106
patch, 104–8
preparation, 104
side seam, 104, 107–8
zipped in Vinyl or leather, 106

Preparation for dressmaking, 47–51
cutting out, 50–1
material, 48–50
special layouts, 48–50
tacking and marking, 51

Pressing, 60–5
equipment, 45–6, 60–1
general hints, 61
how to press, 61–4
what to press, 61–4

Raincoat, coverall from, 116

Remnants, 48–50
planning special layouts, 48–50

Ruler, 42

Scissors, 40, 50–1

Seams, 55–6
pressing, 63
types, 55–6

Sewing gauge, 43
machine, 39

Shirring, 70

Shirt for parties, 155
Spanish-style, 149

Skirt, easy dirndl, 116–17
kilt, 138–40
pleated, 33

Sleeves, 87–94
adapting pattern, 36
bishop, 36

159

Sleeves, (*contd*)
   cuffs, 92–4
   dolman, 17
   faced slit opening, 92
   finishing, 91–2
   magyar or kimono, 87, 90–1
   plain or set-in, 87–9
   raglan, 17, 36, 87, 89–90
   zipped opening, 93

Slip, foundation, 144–5

Smocking, 68–9
   honeycomb stitch, 69
   rope or cable, 69

Sticky tape, 43

Stiletto, 43

Styles, 17–18
   choosing the best, 17–18

Sun outfit and 'angel tops', 154

Tabard, 153
   adapting pattern, 34

Tacking, 51–3
   tailor tacking, 52–3

Tailor's chalk, 42–3

Tailoring, 127–33
   collar, 130–1
   collar facings, 131
   hem and sleeve ends, 132
   interfacing, 128–9
   lining, 132–3
   materials, 127–8
   pad stitching, 129–30
   sleeves, 131–2

Tape measure, 41
   steel measure, 42

Thimble, 42

Thread outlining, 54–5

Threads, 42

Toddler's clothes, 36–8
   dungarees, 117–18
   special requirements, 36–8

Toggles, 126

Tops, 'angel', 154

Towel turnabouts, 115–16

Tracing wheel, 44, 54

Triangle and set square, 43

Trousers, 35–6, 118–20
   adapting pattern, 35–6
   adding turn-ups and pockets, 156
   corduroy, 120
   lengthening the back, 29
   measuring, 15–17
   older child's, 118–20
   shortening the back, 29

Tucks, 70, 73

Tweezers, 44

Unpicking tool, 43

Waistcoat, adapting pattern, 34

Yoke, double, 142
   high, 32

Zippers, 95–8
   central method, 96–7
   lapped method, 97
   set into slot, 98
   with simulated leather, 98